THE UNSETTLED DEBT:
EXAMINING THE RESPONSIBILITY
OF THE WORLD TOWARDS
THE DEMOCRATIC REPUBLIC OF CONGO

Does the world owe DRC?

Yemi Adesina

Azurite (Copper) Native Copper Malachite (Copper) Quartz (Silicon) Gold Ore

Graphite

Bauxite (Aluminium)

Hydrocarbons Pegmatite (Rare Earth Elements) Stibnite (Antimony)

Congo minerals in your mobile phone

"Many blame the DRC and other developing countries for their poverty and say, "What's wrong with you? Why don't you govern yourselves properly?". We don't reflect on the real history of the DRC ..... Instead, we point fingers at these countries

Yet we don't seem to remember or want to remember that starting around 1870, King Leopold of Belgium created a slave colony in the Congo that lasted for around 40 years. Then the government of Belgium ran the colony for another 50 years. In 1961, after the independence of the DRC, the CIA then assassinated the DRC's first popular leader, Patrice Lumumba, and installed a US-backed dictator, Mobutu Sese Seko, for roughly the next 30 years. And in recent years, Glencore and other multinational companies suck out the DRC's cobalt without paying a level of royalties and taxes". We simply don't reflect on the real history of the DRC and other poor countries struggling to escape from poverty. Instead, we point fingers at these countries and say, "What's wrong with you? Why don't you govern yourselves properly?"

—Jeffrey Sachs' speech at the U.N. Food Systems Pre-Summit

CONTENTS

6

Apologia

There are bound to be — only a few, I hope — errors and omissions, and I apologise in advance. No man knows it all, especially me! And you learn more as you get older. One good thing that comes with age is that you are happy to confess when you don't know and pass the inquiry on to a specialist who probably does.

This book is dedicated to hardworking, patient, enthusiastic, generally under-rewarded, and underappreciated people of Africa, those at home and in the diaspora and everyone interested in the welfare of the continent of Africa.

Acknowledgements

Although one man has written this book, it wouldn't have been possible without the many people who have been so inspirational and whose research and hard work were helpful during its writing.

I thank God Almighty for His grace to research and put my findings into a book.

I also owe much to the many people who have encouraged me to follow my dream. In particular, my late dad, Mr Solomon Olajide Adesina. And to Bola, my wife of 27 years of marriage. I thank her immensely for her undying love, support, and encouragement, which allowed me to travel, research, and practise farming in Africa for many years.

For my two sons, Femi and Seun, whose input as the second-generation African diaspora in the United Kingdom makes the book more relevant to younger Africans. I want to thank them for our lengthy chats and the healthy debates that lasted late into the night and early mornings to gather their perspectives on specific topics. I firmly believe their generation and those following beyond will move Africa further into the future.

Many people influenced me to start learning about Africa. Some of them I have met in person, and some I know through their teachings, lectures, training, research books and journals. Coming from all walks of life, the variety of sources, expertise and professions assisted me in approaching the issue from different perspectives, adding much value to this book.

My inspirations were Pastor Matthew Ashimolowo, the late Dr Myles Munro, Dr Mensah Otabil, and Bishop Tudor Bismark. These pastors spent a lot of time teaching and believing Africa could improve.

I am greatly indebted to Dr Toyin Falola, an African historian, Dr Howard Nicholas, an economist and researcher at Erasmus University Rotterdam, and Jeffrey D. Sachs et al. for their input on the impact of geography. I am further indebted to Walter Rodney *for How Europe Underdeveloped Africa*. Finally, I thank Yemi Adeyemi, the founder of ThinkAfrica.net.

The Author

Mr Yemi Adesina is the founder of Boyd Agro-Allied Ltd, one of the largest pig farms in Nigeria. He is also the CEO of Pristine Integrated Farm Resources Ltd, a non-profit organisation registered in Africa to promote youth and rural empowerment, alleviate poverty in Africa through education, and improve the productivity and livelihood of farmers from subsistence to commercial farming in Africa.

He is a social worker, a seasoned farmer and a prolific trainer. He posted 150 videos on YouTube (papayemo1) covering farming and African History. Over 2.5 million viewers watched the videos in over 36 countries, making it one of the most-watched videos on YouTube from an African perspective.

He is the author of *"Why Africa Cannot Feed Itself and the Way Forward"*, *"Profitable Pig Farming: A Step-by-Step Guide to Commercial Pig Farming from an African Perspective"*, *"What the Ancient African Knew"*, *"Does the World Need Africa"* and *"Nigeria: A Complex Nation at a Crossroads in Africa and the World"*, Mr Yemi posted 150 videos on YouTube (*papayemo1*) covering African history and farming watched by over 2.5 million viewers.

Mr Yemi, a diaspora, emigrated to the United Kingdom in 1991. He studied and worked for 20 years and earned his Master's in Business Administration and Master's in Social Work in the United Kingdom. In 2010, he emigrated to Nigeria to contribute to Nigeria's food production.

Scope of the book

The Democratic Republic of the Congo (DRC) is a country that has captured the world's attention for decades. With its vast natural resources, strategic location in central Africa, and rich cultural heritage, the DRC has the potential to be one of the continent's leading nations. However, the country has also been plagued by political instability, economic underdevelopment, and humanitarian crises for decades.

This book seeks to answer whether the world owes the DRC and, if so, what role it should play in supporting the country's development. To answer this question, we will explore the DRC's history, analyze its current state, examine its challenges, and consider the potential for democratic reform and sustainable development.

This book is based on extensive research and analysis by the author, who has utilised various sources, including academic research, government reports, and reports from experts and stakeholders.

The scope of this book is to explore the potential of the DRC to become a stable and prosperous democracy that can contribute to regional and global development. We will examine the country's challenges and opportunities, as well as the role that the international community can play in supporting its development.

The history of the DRC is complex and multi-faceted, with roots dating back to the pre-colonial era. The country has experienced periods of slavery, colonisation, dictatorship, and war, which have left deep scars on its society and institutions. The DRC has also been the site of some of the deadliest conflicts in modern history, resulting in the loss of millions of lives.

The DRC's significance in Africa and the world is linked to its vast natural resources, including minerals such as cobalt, copper, and gold, as well as its strategic location in central Africa. Due to its ongoing challenges, the country's potential as a leading economic and political power in the region and the continent has yet to be fully realised.

The following chapters will explore the DRC's history, current state, challenges, and prospects. We will examine the potential for democratic reform, sustainable development, and the international community's role in supporting the country's development. By doing so, we hope to comprehensively analyse the DRC's potential to become a stable and prosperous democracy that can contribute to regional and global development.

By comprehensively analysing the DRC's significance and challenges, this book aims to raise awareness of its importance in global affairs and spark discussions about its future. The book will appeal to scholars, policymakers, and anyone interested in understanding the complex dynamics of African international relations and development.

By delving into the Congo's unique position as one of the world's largest suppliers of minerals crucial to the global technology and energy industries, this book will show that the country's influence extends far beyond its borders. Additionally, the book will explore the environmental challenges facing the Congo and how they are inextricably linked to global climate change.

Ultimately, this book aims to provide readers with a deeper understanding of the Congo's importance to the world and to stimulate discussion on how the international community can work towards a sustainable future that includes the Congo as a vital player.

This book is intended for individuals interested in African politics, international relations, and environmental studies. It is also a valuable resource for policymakers, academics, researchers, and students seeking to understand the role of the DRC in the global community and the implications of its potential absence.

Ultimately, this book aims to provide an ongoing discussion, thought-provoking and informative analysis of the DRC's role in the world and stimulate discussions on the country's future. I hope that this book will contribute to a better understanding of the DRC's importance and inspire positive action towards its development and stability

Introduction

The Democratic Republic of Congo (DRC) has been a land of great promise, tragedy, hope, despair, progress, and regression. Its vast natural resources, including minerals and agricultural land, have long made it a foreign exploitation and interference target. In contrast, its complex ethnic and political landscape has contributed to decades of conflict and instability. Yet, despite these challenges, the people of the DRC have persevered, fighting for their rights and future.

This book explores whether the world owes a debt to the DRC. We examine the country's complex history, including its experiences of slavery, colonization, exploitation, and conflict, and consider how these factors have contributed to its ongoing struggles with poverty, underdevelopment, and political instability. We also explore the international community's role in shaping the DRC's past and present and consider the implications of these legacies for the country's future.

We argue that the world indeed owes a debt to the DRC, which takes many forms. First and foremost, the legacy of colonization left deep scars on the country and its people. The brutal exploitation of the Congolese people by European powers, particularly under King Leopold II of Belgium, is a stain on the history of humanity and continues to impact the country today.

Furthermore, the DRC is owed a debt for its ongoing struggles with conflict and instability. The wars that have plagued the country have claimed millions of lives and left millions more displaced, leading to widespread suffering and human rights abuses. Many of these conflicts was fueled by external interests, including multinational corporations seeking to exploit the country's resources and neighbouring countries seeking to exert political influence over the region.

Additionally, the DRC is owed a debt for the environmental damage caused by the extraction of its natural resources. The country's minerals, including cobalt, copper, and diamonds, are essential to the global economy. Still, the extraction of these resources has come at a great cost to the environment, leading to deforestation, pollution, and the destruction of wildlife habitats.

In this book, we explore these various debts owed to the DRC and consider the implications of these debts for the country's present and future. We also explore how the international community can work to address these debts, including through efforts to promote sustainable development, support peace-building and conflict resolution, and protect human rights and the environment. Ultimately, we argue that by acknowledging and addressing these debts, the world can help build a more just and equitable future for the people of the DRC and humanity as a whole.

1. Geography

1.1. THE LOCATION

The Democratic Republic of the Congo is located in central Africa. Congo is bounded to the north by the Central African Republic and South Sudan; to the east by Uganda, Rwanda, Burundi, and Tanzania; to the southeast by Zambia; and to the southwest by Angola. To the west are the country's short Atlantic coastline, the Angolan exclave of Cabinda, and Congo (Brazzaville). The country is the second largest on the continent; only Algeria is larger, but it only has a 25-mile (40-km) coastline on the Atlantic Ocean. The rest of the country is otherwise landlocked. The capital, Kinshasa, is located on the Congo River, about 320 miles (515 km) from its mouth. The largest city in central Africa serves as the country's official administrative, economic, and cultural centre. The country is often referred to by its acronym, the DRC, or called Congo (Kinshasa), with the capital added parenthetically to distinguish it from the other Congo republic, officially called the Republic of the Congo and is often referred to as Congo (Brazzaville).

Map of Congo. Source *www.bbc.com*

The entire length of the Congo River is 2,720 miles and flows into the Atlantic Ocean. DRC gained independence from Belgium in 1960. From 1971 to 1997, the country was officially the Republic of Zaire, a change made by then-ruler Gen. Mobutu Sese Seko to give the country what he thought was a more authentic African name. "Zaire" is a variation of a term meaning "great river" in local African languages; like the country's current name, it refers to the Congo River, which drains a large basin that lies mostly in the republic. Unlike Zaire, however, the name Congo has origins in the colonial period, when Europeans identified the river with the kingdom of the Kongo people, who live near its mouth. In 1997, the country's name before 1971, the Democratic Republic of the Congo, was reinstated. Congo is rich in natural resources. It boasts vast deposits of industrial diamonds, cobalt, and copper; one of the largest forest reserves in Africa; and about half of the hydroelectric potential of the continent.

1.2. THE LAND

The Democratic Republic of the Congo (DRC) is a vast and diverse country located in the heart of Africa. It is the second-largest country in Africa, covering an area of approximately 2.3 million square kilometres. The land and vegetation of the DRC are equally diverse, ranging from dense rainforests to vast savannas, from high mountain peaks to broad river valleys.

The DRC is located in the Congo Basin, home to one of the world's largest rainforests, the Congo Rainforest. The Congo Rainforest is the second-largest tropical rainforest in the world after the Amazon, covering approximately 1.5 million square kilometres. It is a vital ecosystem that provides a habitat for a vast array of plant and animal species, including endangered gorillas, chimpanzees, and forest elephants.

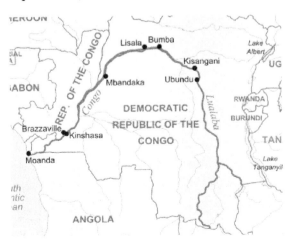

Congo River. Source *www.re-tawon.com*

The Congo River, one of the world's largest rivers, flows through the heart of the DRC. The deepest river in the world is the Congo River in Africa. At its deepest point, it reaches a depth of 720 feet. That makes it almost five times deeper than Sydney Harbour, 197 feet, the world's deepest natural harbour. The river is approximately 4,700 kilometres long, and its basin covers an area of over 4 million square kilometres. The river is a vital source of water and transportation for the people living along its banks, and it is also home to a diverse array of fish species.

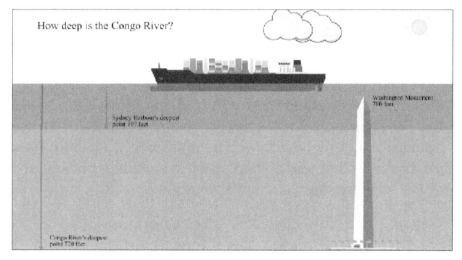

How deep is Congo River. Source: *www.quora.com*

The eastern part of the DRC is home to a series of mountain ranges, including the Rwenzori Mountains, the Virunga Mountains, and the Mitumba Mountains. High peaks and steep slopes characterize these mountains, with dense forests and grasslands. The Virunga Mountains, in particular, are home to the critically endangered mountain gorilla.

In addition to rainforests, mountains, and rivers, the DRC also has vast savannas, particularly in the south and east of the country. Tall grasses, scattered trees, and various wildlife, including antelopes, zebras, and giraffes, characterize these savannas.

DRC Gorilla. Source: *www.Safari.com*

1.3. **THE CLIMATE**

The climate of the Democratic Republic of the Congo (DRC) is predominantly tropical, with high temperatures and humidity throughout the year. However, due to the country's vast size and varied terrain, there is significant regional variation in climate patterns. The equator passes through the northern part of the country, so the northern regions experience a hot and humid equatorial climate. The average temperature in this region is around 25-27 degrees Celsius, with high levels of rainfall throughout the year. The region experiences two rainy seasons, from March to May and from September to November, with a brief dry season in July and August. Towards the south, the climate becomes less equatorial, with a transition to a tropical climate. This region, which includes the capital city of Kinshasa, experiences more distinct seasons, with a wet season from

October to May and a dry season from June to September. Average temperatures in this region range from 22 to 28 degrees Celsius, with higher temperatures during the dry season. The country's eastern part, including the Virunga Mountains and Lake Kivu, experiences a subtropical climate due to its higher elevation. The western part of the country, which borders the Atlantic Ocean, experiences a maritime climate characterized by high levels of rainfall throughout the year. The region's temperatures are moderated by ocean breezes, with average temperatures ranging from 21 to 27 degrees Celsius.

Despite the variation in regional climates, the DRC is susceptible to extreme weather events, including floods, droughts, and landslides. These events can cause significant damage to infrastructure, homes, and agriculture, threatening the lives and livelihoods of people living in affected areas.

The land and vegetation of the DRC are vital to the country's economy and its people. The rainforests provide timber and other forest products, while the savannas are home to agriculture and livestock farming. The Congo River is an important transportation route for goods and people, providing hydroelectric power to the country.

The Congo Basin rainforest in Central Africa is Earth's African lung. With an area as big as Western Europe, it is the second-largest rainforest in the world. It absorbs 4% of global carbon dioxide emissions every year, offsetting more than the whole African continent's annual emissions. This represents about 1.1 billion tonnes of carbon dioxide per. The Basin is also Africa's thermostat as it regulates rainfall patterns, critical to Sahel and beyond dry areas.

However, the land and vegetation of the DRC have been under threat in recent years. Deforestation, caused by logging and agriculture, is a significant problem in the country. Between 2000 and 2010, the DRC lost approximately 1.3 million hectares of forest yearly. Deforestation threatens numerous plant and animal habitats and contributes to global climate change by releasing carbon dioxide into the atmosphere.

In addition to deforestation, the DRC's land and vegetation are also threatened by mining activities. The country is rich in minerals, including copper, cobalt, gold, and diamonds, often extracted through destructive methods that damage the surrounding environment. Deforestation can lead to soil erosion, water pollution, and the destruction of wildlife habitats.

The DRC's government has taken steps to address these environmental challenges. In 2002, the country adopted a forestry law to protect its forests and promote sustainable forest management. The government has also established a protected area network, including national parks and wildlife reserves, to conserve the country's biodiversity. The DRC is also a signatory to the Paris Agreement on climate change, which commits the country to reduce its greenhouse gas emissions.

In conclusion, the land and vegetation of the DRC are incredibly diverse and essential to the country's ecology, culture, and economy. However, they face numerous threats, including deforestation and mining activities. Understanding and protecting these ecosystems is essential to the DRC's future and its people's. Addressing these challenges will require the government to balance economic development with environmental protection and work collaboratively with local communities, civil society, and the private sector. With concerted efforts and collective action, the DRC's land and vegetation can be protected and sustainably managed for the benefit of present and future generations.

1.4. WHY DOES THE DRC HAVE SUCH ABUNDANT MINERAL RESOURCES?

The Democratic Republic of the Congo (DRC) is known for its vast mineral resources, which include copper, cobalt, gold, diamonds, tin, and coltan. The country has some of the largest mineral reserves in the world, accounting for a significant portion of global production.

There are several reasons why the DRC has such abundant mineral resources. One is the country's unique geological history. The DRC is part of the African Copperbelt, which extends across Zambia and into the Katanga region of the DRC. This region was formed around 500 million years ago when sedimentary rocks were deposited in a shallow sea. The rocks were later uplifted, folded, and faulted, creating a complex geological structure that contains significant mineral deposits.

Another reason for the DRC's mineral wealth is its location in the heart of Africa. The country's central location and extensive river network made it a hub for trade and transportation in pre-colonial times. This facilitated the movement of goods, including minerals, across the continent. It also made the region a target for foreign exploitation, as European powers sought to exploit its resources for their own economic gain.

The DRC's mineral wealth has also been a source of conflict and instability. The country's long colonization, exploitation, and conflict history has made developing a sustainable and equitable mineral sector difficult. In recent years, the government has addressed these challenges, including reforming the legal and regulatory framework for mining, promoting transparency and accountability, and improving social and environmental standards.

2. A Brief History of the DRC

2.1. PRE-COLONIAL

The Democratic Republic of the Congo (DRC) has a rich and complex history that dates back to the pre-colonial era. The region that now makes up the DRC was once inhabited by various ethnic groups who lived in different kingdoms and empires. It was home to various ethnic groups, including the Luba, Kuba, and Kongo, with distinct cultures and political systems.

The earliest known kingdom in the region that now makes up the DRC was the Kingdom of Kongo. This kingdom was founded in the late 14th century by a ruler named Lukeni lua Nimi. The Kingdom of Kongo was a highly centralized state with a strong monarchy and a sophisticated bureaucracy. It had a powerful army and an extensive system of trade routes that connected it to other parts of Africa and beyond. The Kingdom of Kongo was also known for its cultural and artistic achievements, including its distinctive sculpture and music.

João I of Kongo (died 1509), alias Nzinga a Nkuwu or Nkuwu Nzinga, was ruler of the Kingdom of Kongo between 1470–1509. He was baptized as João on 3 May 1491 by Portuguese missionaries. Due to his interest in Portugal and its culture, he initiated a major cultural initiative in 1485 upon the arrival of Diogo Cão. Under these conditions, the first Atlantic Creole emerged, forming in Central Africa and Portugal.

João I of Kongo Source: *blogspot.com*

One of these emerging kingdoms was the Luba Kingdom, founded in the 16th century by a ruler named Kongolo. The Luba Kingdom was located in the southern part of what is now the DRC and was known for its sophisticated political system, which was based on a complex hierarchy of chiefs and rulers. The Luba Kingdom was also a major centre of trade and commerce, with its people producing and exchanging ivory, copper, salt, and other goods.

Another significant kingdom in the region was the Lunda Kingdom, founded in the 17th century by a ruler named Mwata Yamvo. The Lunda Kingdom was located in the eastern part of what is now the DRC and was known for its strong military and political organization. The Lunda Kingdom also had a sophisticated trade system, which included exchanging ivory, salt, and other goods with neighbouring kingdoms and empires.

In addition to these kingdoms, there were also smaller chiefdoms and states throughout the region, each with its own distinct cultures and political systems. These smaller states often engaged in trade and conflict with one another, leading to a complex and dynamic political landscape.

2.2. DRC ENCOUNTER WITH THE EUROPEANS

Portugal was one of the first European powers to establish contact with the peoples of the Congo region in the late 15th century. Initially, Portuguese interactions with the Congo were limited to trade in ivory, pepper, and other goods, but they became more complex and sometimes violent.

In the early 16th century, Portuguese traders established a series of trading posts along the Congo River, including São Salvador (present-day Mbanza-Kongo), which became the capital of the Kongo Kingdom. The Portuguese significantly impacted the Kongo Kingdom, introducing new crops and livestock, firearms, and Christianity. They also played a role in the political affairs of the kingdom, supporting some rulers over others and sometimes intervening militarily in conflicts.

Despite these early contacts, Portugal's relations with the Congo were often fraught with tension and conflict. In the mid-16th century, the Portuguese launched a series of wars against the Kingdom of Ndongo, a powerful state in northern Angola and southern DRC. The wars were driven by the Portuguese desire for slaves, which they sold to the growing sugar plantations of Brazil and the Caribbean. The wars devastated the peoples of Ndongo, with many being killed, enslaved, or forced to flee their homes.

In the late 19th and early 20th centuries, Portugal's presence in the Congo became more limited as other European powers, such as Belgium and France, established colonies there. Portugal maintained some influence in Angola, which borders the DRC to the west, but its interactions with the DRC were largely limited to trade and occasional diplomatic contacts.

The battles of Mbumbi and the Battle of Mbandi Kasi were two significant military conflicts that the Portuguese had with what is now the Democratic Republic of Congo during the early 17th century.

Battle of Mbumbi

The Battle of Mbumbi was a military engagement between forces of the Portuguese and the Kingdom of Kongo in 1622. Although the Portuguese were victorious, the battle impeded the Kingdom of Kongo from expelling the Portuguese from their territory.

Portuguese Angola was established in 1575 to reward the Portuguese for helping the Kingdom of Kongo defeat the Jagas, who invaded the realm in 1568. The Portuguese were rewarded by the slaves that emerged from the chaos. In 1621, 20,000 Portuguese fought against the 3,000 armies led by Paulo Afonso, the Duke of Mbamba and destroyed the commercial town of Bumbi. After the battle, the Portuguese pillaged Mbumbi and took many slaves from the battle. The Portuguese allies and the Imbangala soldiers eat some of the war prisoners.

Battle of Mbandi Kasi

Pedro II Nkanga a Mvika, a ruler of the kingdom of Kongo, immediately declared the Portuguese an enemy of the state and brought his main army down from Kongo to meet the invaders at Mbanda Kasi. The army of Kongo crushed the Portuguese and the Imbangala and forced them out of Kongo entirely. In the aftermath, anti-Portuguese riots broke out throughout the kingdom and threatened its long-established merchant community. Portuguese were humiliatingly disarmed and forced to give up their clothes.

Battle of Mbumbi. Source: *Wikipedia.com*

Pedro II wrote numerous letters of protest to Rome and the king of Spain (then also the ruler of Portugal). As a result of these letters, João Correia de Sousa, the Portuguese governor, was recalled in disgrace, and 1,200 slaves were returned from Brazil. Pedro was later called the "King of Portuguese".

Today, Portugal's historical interactions with the peoples of the Congo region are remembered for their positive and negative impacts. While the Portuguese introduced new crops and technologies, they also contributed to the slave trade. They were responsible for wars that had long-lasting consequences for the region's people. Understanding this complex legacy is an important part of understanding the history of the Congo and its relations with the wider world.

2.3. ARAB SLAVERY IN DCR

The Arab trans-Saharan slave trade was a significant part of the history of the Democratic Republic of Congo (DRC) and the wider African continent. For centuries, Arab slave traders from the Middle East and North Africa captured and transported millions of Africans across the Sahara and the Indian Ocean to work as slaves.

According to Dr John Alembellah Azumah, in his book: "The Legacy of Arab-Islam in Africa". The Arabs began to invade Africa in large numbers in 749 CE, and they settled in Alexandria, Egypt. In the beginning, the Arabs were mistakenly perceived by Africans as African cousins and were welcomed as saviours from the oppressive rule of Byzantium (Graeco-Roman domination.) The Arabs did not initially force their religion on the African Egyptians, but Qur'an could not be translated into local languages like the Bible. As a result, literacy in Arabic soon spread and was assisted by intermarriages, and Islam soon became the land's religion.

However, in the DRC, the Arab slave trade was particularly devastating. Arab traders primarily drove the slave trade from Zanzibar, who raided villages and captured men, women, and children to sell into slavery. The slave trade profoundly impacted the region's demographics, uprooting entire communities and families tearing apart.

Slavery in the DRC was not limited to the capture and transportation of Africans. Once enslaved, people were subjected to brutal treatment, forced labour, and sexual exploitation. Slaves were used to working on plantations, in mines, and as domestic servants. Slaves were also sold in markets throughout the region, where they were viewed as commodities and traded for goods such as textiles, weapons, and ivory.

Arab Slavery. Source *superstock.com*

The chaos and devastation that followed the Arab invasions finally set up Africa for the intense European slave trade that followed. As the Muslim conquest and religion spread throughout North Africa and across the Sahara into West Africa, Arab hunger to enslave the Africans increased.

The Arab slave trade in the DRC persisted until the late 19th century, when the British finally abolished it. However, its legacy continues to impact the region today. The slave trade disrupted traditional African societies and economies, contributing to the DRC's underdevelopment.

One of the most notorious Arab slave traders is Tippu Tip; in the next section, we will consider his role in Congo Free State.

3. King Leopold of Belgium

3.1. KING LEOPOLD OF BELGIUM AND ARAB SLAVE TRADER TIPPU TIP

Tippu Tip, also known as Tippu Tib, was a notorious Arab slave trader and ivory trader who played a significant role in the subjugation of the Democratic Republic of Congo (DRC) to King Leopold of Belgium. Born in Zanzibar in 1837, Tippu Tip became one of East and Central Africa's wealthiest and most powerful men, amassing a fortune through the slave trade and ivory trade.

Tippu Tip's influence in the Congo region began in the late 19th century when he established a powerful slave-trading network that spanned East Africa and the Congo River Basin. He was instrumental in transporting ivory and slaves from the interior of Africa to the coast, where they were sold to European and Arab traders.

Tippu Tip and Arab Slave trade. Source: *https://aaregistry.org/*

In 1876, Tippu Tip was approached by King Leopold of Belgium, who had ambitions of colonizing the Congo and exploiting its vast natural resources. Leopold was interested in Tippu Tip's extensive knowledge of the Congo region and his ability to navigate the difficult terrain and negotiate with local rulers. In exchange for his services, Leopold promised Tippu Tip a share in the profits from the Congo's resources and guaranteed his protection from other European powers.

Tippu Tip agreed to work with Leopold and played a key role in establishing the Congo Free State, a private colony controlled by Leopold responsible for the Congolese people's forced labour and brutal exploitation. Tippu Tip's knowledge of the local languages and cultures made him an invaluable asset to Leopold's agents, who used him to establish trade relationships and negotiate treaties with local rulers.

Under Tippu Tip's guidance, Leopold's agents established a network of trading posts and military outposts across the Congo, effectively taking control of the region and subjugating the local population. Tippu Tip's influence in the region was so great that he was appointed governor of several provinces, overseeing the forced labour of thousands of Congolese people.

Tippu Tip's involvement in the Congo's colonisation and collaboration with Leopold profoundly impacted the region's history and development. The Congolese people's forced labour and brutal exploitation led to widespread death and suffering, and the country's natural resources were plundered and exported to Europe and the United States. Tippu Tip was complicit in the atrocities committed against the Congolese people.

The story of Tippu Tip and King Leopold's exploitation of the Congo serves as a cautionary tale of the dangers of unchecked power and greed. It highlights the devastating consequences of the slave trade and colonization and the importance of acknowledging and addressing the historical injustices that continue to impact Africa and its people.

In conclusion, Tippu Tip was a powerful and influential figure in East and Central Africa whose involvement in the slave trade and ivory trade contributed to the subjugation of the Congo to King Leopold of Belgium. While Tippu Tip's knowledge of the region and his ability to navigate its difficult terrain were valuable assets to Leopold, his complicity in exploiting the Congolese people cannot be ignored.

3.2. DAVID LIVINGSTONE'S EXPLORATION OF THE DRC

David Livingstone was a Scottish physician, Congregationalist, and pioneer Christian missionary with the London Missionary Society, an explorer in Africa, and one of the most popular British heroes of the late 19th-century Victorian era.

David Livingstone's exploration of the Democratic Republic of Congo (DRC) was part of his broader mission to spread Christianity in Africa. In 1871, he embarked on his final expedition to find the source of the Nile River, which he believed was in the heart of Central Africa. This journey took him through what is now the DRC, and he documented the region's geography and people in his journals.

During his travels, Livingstone encountered various indigenous tribes in the DRC, including the Luba and Lunda kingdoms. He noted their customs, languages, and political structures, which he believed held promise for the region's future development. Livingstone was also horrified by the atrocities committed by Arab slave traders in the DRC, and he saw the region's vast natural resources as a potential source of wealth.

Livingstone's journey through the DRC was difficult and dangerous. He faced hostile tribes, harsh weather, and illness, and his expedition suffered from a lack of supplies and funding. However, he persevered, driven by his belief in the transformative power of Christianity and commerce.

 One of his most famous expeditions was his journey to the Zambezi River, where he discovered Victoria Falls. Livingstone's travels were celebrated in Europe, and he became a household name for his work in previously exploring and mapping uncharted areas of Africa.

It was during his travels that Livingstone first met King Leopold of Belgium, who had ambitions of establishing a Belgian colony in Africa. Leopold recognized the potential of the Congo region and saw it as a valuable source of raw materials and wealth. He sought to establish control over the region, and in 1876, he established the International Association of the Congo, a private organization that aimed to develop and exploit the region's resources.

Leopold recognized the value of Livingstone's reputation and used him as a tool to further his own agenda in the region. Livingstone became a pawn in Leopold's scheme to establish control over the Congo, and Leopold used his influence to shape

Livingstone's opinions and actions. Livingstone was convinced of Leopold's good intentions and saw him as a potential ally in his mission to spread Christianity in Africa.

Livingstone's belief in Leopold's good intentions was misplaced. Leopold's exploitation of the Congo was brutal and exploitative, responsible for millions of Africans' deaths. Under the guise of philanthropy and humanitarianism, Leopold established a system of forced labour and exploitation that enriched himself and his supporters at the expense of the Congolese people.

Livingstone's relationship with Leopold highlights the complex dynamics between explorers, missionaries, and colonial powers in Africa during this period. While Livingstone saw himself as a missionary and humanitarian, his influence and reputation were used to further the agenda of colonial power. Exploiting the Congo was a tragic consequence of these tensions, and it had a lasting impact on the region and its people.

Livingstone's legacy also underscores the importance of understanding the historical context of exploration and colonization. While Livingstone was celebrated in his time for his expeditions and discoveries, his actions and beliefs were shaped by his time's prevailing attitudes and beliefs. He was not immune to the biases and prejudices of his era, and his interactions with the people he encountered during his travels reflect this.

Today, Livingstone's legacy is still felt in Africa and beyond. He remains an important figure in the history of exploration and missionary work, and his influence can be seen in the work of modern-day explorers and humanitarians. However, his relationship with Leopold and the exploitation of the Congo serves as a cautionary tale about the dangers of unchecked colonialism and exploitation. It is a reminder of the importance of respecting the autonomy and dignity of the people and cultures that explorers and missionaries encounter in their travels.

Livingstone died in 1873 before Leopold's true intentions for the Congo were revealed. Had he lived to see the atrocities committed in the name of Leopold's empire, his opinion of Leopold would likely have changed. However, his reputation as a respected explorer and missionary was used to legitimize Leopold's actions and contribute to the exploitation of the Congo.

In conclusion, David Livingstone played a significant role in exploring Africa and spreading Christianity. However, his relationship with King Leopold of Belgium and his misplaced trust in Leopold's intentions contributed to the exploitation of the Congo. Livingstone's legacy is complex, highlighting the tensions between European exploration and exploitation of Africa during the 19th century.

3.3. HENRY MORTON STANLEY

Henry Morton Stanley was a British explorer and journalist best known for exploring the Congo Basin in what is now the Democratic Republic of Congo (DRC). In the late 1800s, Stanley embarked on a series of expeditions to explore and map the region, which was then largely uncharted by Europeans.

One of Stanley's most famous expeditions was his search for the missing Scottish explorer, Dr David Livingstone, who had not been heard from for several years. In 1871, Stanley set out to find Livingstone and eventually located him in Tanzania. This encounter gave Stanley fame and credibility as an explorer and led to his appointment by King Leopold II of Belgium to lead an expedition to explore the Congo River.

Henry Morton Stanley

Henry Morton Stanley is
a photograph by Granger

In 1874, Stanley began his exploration of the Congo River, which he believed held great potential for trade and commerce. Stanley's expedition faced many challenges, including disease, hostile tribes, and difficult terrain. However, he persevered and successfully navigated the river to its source, opening up a new route for trade and commerce in the region.

Stanley's exploration of the Congo Basin was not without controversy. His partnership with King Leopold II of Belgium led to the establishment of the Congo Free State, a private colony owned and controlled by the King. The exploitation and abuse of the Congolese people by the King's agents in the Congo Free State is widely regarded as one of the most brutal episodes in the history of European colonialism in Africa.

3.4. KING LEOPOLD

> *"Evangelize the niggers so that they stay forever in submission to the white colonialists and never revolt against the restraints they are undergoing. Recite daily — 'happy are those who are weeping because the kingdom of God is for them.' Convert always the blacks by using the whip. Keep their women in nine months of submission to work freely for us. Force them to pay you in a sign of recognition — goats, chickens or eggs — every time you visit their villages. And make sure that niggers never become rich. Sing every day that the rich can't enter heaven. Make them pay tax each week at Sunday mass. Use the money supposed for the poor, to build flourishing business centers. Institute a confessional system, which allows you to be good detectives denouncing any black with a different consciousness, contrary to the decision-maker. Teach the niggers to forget their heroes and to adore only ours. Never present a chair to a black that comes to visit you. Don't give him more than one cigarette. Never invite him for dinner even if he gives you a chicken every time you arrive at his house."*
>
> *— King Leopold II (Belgian)*

King Leopold II of Belgium is a controversial figure in the history of the Democratic Republic of Congo (DRC). During his reign from 1865 to 1909, Leopold was responsible for some of the most brutal atrocities in the history of European colonialism in Africa, resulting in the deaths of millions of Congolese people.

As a philanthropist eager to bring the benefits of Christianity, Western civilization, and commerce to African natives, Leopold hosted an international conference of explorers and geographers at the royal palace in Brussels in 1876. Several years later, he hired the explorer Henry Morton Stanley as his man in Africa. For five years, Stanley travelled up and down the immense waterways of the Congo River basin, setting up trading posts, building roads, and persuading local chiefs—almost illiterate—to sign treaties with Leopold.

King Leopold II. Source *www.bbc.co.uk*

King Leopold II was a prominent figure in the European colonial scramble for Africa and was keen on acquiring territory to expand his influence and wealth. The success of the British in India and the French in Algeria sparked his interest in Africa. He saw Africa as an opportunity to establish Belgium as a global power. King Leopold persuaded all the major nations of Western Europe to recognize the modern-day Democratic Republic of the Congo as his personal property. He called it État Indépendant du Congo, the Congo Free State.

In 1876, Leopold II founded the International African Association, a philanthropic organization that was ostensibly created to promote humanitarian and scientific research in Africa. However, the real purpose of the association was to provide a cover for Leopold's plans to colonize the Congo Basin. The association set up a series of trading posts in the region, ostensibly to facilitate trade with the local population, but in reality to establish a foothold in the area.

In 1884, at the Berlin Conference, European powers met to divide Africa amongst themselves. Leopold II persuaded the other European powers to recognize his claim to the Congo Basin as a personal possession rather than a Belgian possession. The Congo Free State was created, and Leopold II became its ruler, completely controlling its land and resources.

The king then embarked on an ultimately successful effort to make a vast fortune from his new possession. Initially, he was most interested in ivory, a material that was greatly valued in the days before plastics because it could be carved into a great variety of shapes—statuettes, jewellery, piano keys, false teeth, and more.

By the early 1890s, a new source of riches had appeared. A worldwide rubber boom was under way, kicked off by the invention of the inflatable bicycle tire and spurred on by the rise of the automobile and the use of rubber in industrial belts and coating for the telephone and the telegraph wires. People rushed to sow rubber trees throughout the tropics, but those plants could take many years to reach maturity. One lucrative source of wild rubber was the Landolphia vines in the great Central African rainforest, and no one owned more of that area than Leopold. Detachments of his 19,000-man private army, the Force Publique, would march into a village and hold the women hostage, forcing the men to scatter into the rainforest and gather a monthly quota of wild rubber. As the price of rubber soared, the quotas increased, and as vines near a village were drained dry, men desperate to free their wives and daughters would have to walk days or weeks to find new vines to tap.

Individuals who failed to meet rubber quotas faced severe punishment, including mutilation or death.

Leopold II's reign over the Congo Free State was brutal and exploitative. He commissioned the construction of a vast network of railroads and infrastructure projects, all built by forced labour. The indigenous population was forced to work long hours for little pay, and many were subjected to violence and torture.

Father stares at the hand and foot of his five-year-old, severed as a punishment for failing to make the daily rubber quota, Belgian Congo, 1904. The henchman was showing off the amputated hand.

Many of the women hostages starved, and many of the male rubber gatherers were worked to death. Tens, possibly hundreds, of thousands of Congolese fled their villages to avoid being impressed as forced labourers, and they sought refuge deep in the forest, where there was little food and shelter. Tens of thousands of others were shot down in failed rebellions against the regime. One particularly notorious practice grew out of the suppression of those rebellions. To prove that he had not wasted bullets—or, worse yet, saved them for use in a mutiny—for each bullet expended, a Congolese soldier of the Force Publique had to present to his white officer the severed hand of a rebel killed. Baskets of severed hands thus resulted from expeditions against rebels. If a soldier fired at someone and missed or used a bullet to shoot a game, he sometimes cut off the hand of a living victim to show it to his office.

EXECUTION OF SLAVES BY THE WAKUTI, NEAR EQUATOR STATION.

An illustration from HM Stanley's (1885). Source: Wikimedia Commons

With women as hostages and men forced to tap rubber, few non-disabled adults were left to hunt, fish, and cultivate crops. Millions of Congolese then found themselves suffering near-famine, which made them vulnerable to diseases they otherwise might have survived. Furthermore, as in any society where men and women are separated, traumatized, or in flight as refugees, the birth rate drops precipitously.

This system led to the deaths of millions of Congolese, and the forced labour system became known as the "red rubber" system.

Many historians have contended whether it is possible that Leopold II, a fairly observant Belgian Catholic, really did want to introduce his new chattel to Jesus. But he did this in the most literal and ruthless way possible: by killing a huge number of them and making life generally unbearable for the rest as they labored to dig up gold, hunted to kill elephants for ivory.

Regular flogging

African girl in a human zoo, Belgium, 1958

African girl in a zoo.
Source: *www.bbc.co.uk*

The brutality of Leopold II's rule in the Congo Free State was eventually exposed by a number of journalists and human rights activists, including E.D. Morel and Roger Casement, who worked to raise awareness of the atrocities being committed in the region. Their efforts led to widespread international condemnation of Leopold's regime, and in 1908 the Belgian government took control of the Congo Free State, renaming it the Belgian Congo.

The legacy of Leopold II's rule in the Congo Free State is one of exploitation, violence, and suffering. The country's resources were extracted to benefit Belgium and Leopold's personal wealth, and millions of Congolese were subjected to forced labour and brutal violence. The effects of this period of colonization can still be felt in the DRC today as the country struggles to overcome the economic, political, and social challenges resulting from decades of exploitation and oppression.

Under Leopold's rule, the Congolese people were subjected to brutal forced labour, starvation, and violence. The King's agents, known as the Force Publique, were given carte blanche to carry out horrific acts of violence against the Congolese people, including amputations, rape, and murder.

The consequences of Leopold's brutality in the DRC were devastating. Estimates suggest that as many as 10 million Congolese people died due to his policies, including the widespread use of forced labour, violence, and disease. The Congolese people were left impoverished, traumatized, and with a legacy of discrimination and marginalization that persists to this day.

The legacy of Leopold's cruelty in the DRC is complex and multi-faceted. His brutality contributed to the region's underdevelopment, perpetuated racial and economic inequality, and traumatized generations of Congolese people. However, his atrocities also raised international awareness about the injustices of European colonialism in Africa, leading to the eventual decolonization of the continent.

Today, the DRC remains one of the poorest and most unstable countries in the world, and the effects of Leopold's brutality continue to be felt. However, efforts to promote justice, reconciliation, and development in the region continue, and there is hope that the country can eventually move past the legacy of its colonial past.

3.5. THE BELGIAN GOVERNMENT'S RULE OF DRC

After the international community condemned the atrocities committed by King Leopold II in Congo, he was forced to turn over the land to the Belgian government in 1908. However, Belgian rule brought challenges and problems to the Congo instead of improving the situation.

Belgium's primary objective was to maximize profits from the region's natural resources, particularly rubber and copper. To achieve this, the Belgian colonial administration implemented a forced labour and taxation system called the "Congo Free State" system. Congolese were forced to work in mines, plantations, and other industries to generate revenue for the state.

The brutal forced labour and taxation system led to widespread abuse and exploitation of the Congolese people. Belgian officials and private companies subjected the Congolese to torture, mutilation, and murder to increase profits. Congolese were forced to collect rubber and other natural resources for export at the expense of their health, welfare, and families.

Belgium 'human zoo' Source: *www.bbc.co.uk*

The Belgian government also implemented a policy of indirect rule, whereby they relied on traditional leaders and chiefs to maintain control over the population. This system was used to exploit and manipulate local communities, pitting different groups against each other for the benefit of the Belgian colonial administration.

In addition, the Belgian government's policies favoured a small group of Congolese elites who received preferential treatment and education access. At the same time, most of the population was left illiterate and impoverished.

Despite the widespread exploitation and violence of the colonial period, there were also some positive developments. The Belgians built infrastructure, such as roads and railways, which helped improve the country's transportation and trade. They also established schools and hospitals, improving education and healthcare access.

However, these positive developments were overshadowed by the widespread suffering and exploitation of the Congolese people during the colonial period. The legacy of the colonial period can still be seen in the country's political and social dynamics today, and it remains a source of controversy and debate.

In conclusion, the Belgian colonial period of the Democratic Republic of Congo was marked by widespread exploitation, violence, and repression. The Belgian authorities' forced labour system, taxation, and divide-and-rule policies devastated the Congolese people. The legacy of this period can still be seen in the country's political and social dynamics today.

4. Independence

4.1. THE CONGO CRISIS AND INDEPENDENCE

The exploitation and abuse of the Congolese people during the colonial era led to a strong sense of resentment and mistrust towards the Belgian government and other Western powers. This would set the stage for future conflicts and instability in the Congo, even after it gained independence from Belgium in 1960.

The Congo Crisis was a period of political turmoil and violence in the Democratic Republic of Congo (DRC) between 1960 and 1965. It was triggered by the country's sudden and tumultuous independence from Belgium, and it had far-reaching consequences for the political and economic development of the DRC.

The Congo had been under Belgian colonial rule since the late 19th century, and during this time, the country's resources had been ruthlessly exploited for the benefit of the colonial power. The Congolese people had little say in their affairs and few opportunities to develop their economic or political institutions. This situation came to a head in the late 1950s and early 1960s, as nationalist movements in the Congo began to agitate for greater autonomy and independence.

In 1960, the Belgian government agreed to grant the Congo independence, but it did so in a hasty and poorly planned manner. Few Congolese leaders were prepared to govern the country, and the Belgian colonial authorities had done little to prepare the country for the transition to independence. As a result, the new Congolese government was weak and divided, and it struggled to assert control over the country's many regions and ethnic groups.

The Congo Crisis quickly escalated into a violent and chaotic conflict. There were numerous secessionist movements as various regions, and ethnic groups sought to break away from the central government. Some international actors became involved in the conflict, including the United States, the Soviet Union, and other African countries.

The crisis had a devastating impact on the Congolese people. The country was plunged into chaos and violence, and thousands of people were killed or displaced. The economy suffered greatly, and the country's infrastructure was damaged. Additionally, the crisis helped entrench a culture of corruption and authoritarianism that continues to affect the DRC today.

Eventually, the crisis was brought to an end through international intervention. In 1965, the United Nations established a peacekeeping force in the Congo, which helped stabilize the situation and end the worst violence. However, the crisis's long-term impact on the DRC's political and economic development has been profound.

Today, the DRC remains one of the world's poorest and most unstable countries, and the Congo Crisis continues to cast a long shadow over the country's politics and society. The crisis was a stark reminder of newly independent African nations' challenges after colonialism, and it underscored the importance of building strong, inclusive political institutions to promote stability and development.

One of the most notable consequences of the Congo Crisis was the rise of authoritarianism in the country. In the years following the crisis, the government of the DRC became increasingly repressive, with political opposition being suppressed and civil society being tightly controlled. This had a chilling effect on the development of democratic institutions in the country and created a culture of fear and mistrust that has persisted to this day.

Another consequence of the Congo Crisis was the emergence of resource-based conflict in the DRC. During the crisis, many factions fought to control the country's valuable mineral resources, such as diamonds, gold, and copper. This led to a proliferation of armed groups, some of which continue to operate in the DRC today. The struggle for control over these resources has been a significant source of instability in the country and has fueled violence and conflict for decades.

Finally, the Congo Crisis highlighted the challenges of building a unified national identity in a country with diverse ethnic and linguistic groups. The crisis was, in many ways, a product of the deep-seated divisions and tensions within Congolese society. It underscored the need for inclusive and participatory forms of governance that could help bridge these divides. Unfortunately, the legacy of the crisis has been one of fragmentation and disunity, with different regions and ethnic groups often pursuing their interests at the expense of the broader national interest.

In conclusion, the Congo Crisis was a pivotal moment in the history of the DRC, and it had far-reaching consequences for the political and economic development of the country. The crisis highlighted the challenges of building strong and inclusive political institutions in the wake of colonialism, and it underscored the importance of addressing underlying divisions and tensions within society. Today, the DRC remains a distraught country. Still, there are signs of hope as civil society groups and reform-minded politicians work to address the legacies of the past and build a more stable and prosperous future.

4.2. THE RISE AND FALL OF PATRICE LUMUMBA

Patrice Lumumba was one of the most important figures in the history of the Democratic Republic of Congo (DRC). He rose to power during a time of great political upheaval in the country, and a strong commitment to democracy, nationalism, and pan-Africanism characterized his leadership. However, his time in power was short-lived, as he was overthrown in a coup just months after he became the country's first democratically elected Prime Minister. Lumumba's rise and fall is a complex story that sheds light on the challenges of post-colonial governance and the role of outside powers in shaping the destiny of African nations.

Lumumba was born in 1925 in the Kasai region of what is now the DRC. He grew up in a Catholic family and received a good education, eventually becoming a postal clerk in the colonial government. However, he quickly became disillusioned with the injustices of the colonial system, and he began to speak out against it. In the 1950s, he joined the Congolese National Movement (MNC), a nationalist organization that advocated for the independence of the Congo.

After years of struggle, the Congo finally achieved independence from Belgium in 1960. Lumumba was elected Prime Minister of the new country and set about trying to build a stable and prosperous nation. However, outside powers quickly challenged his leadership, including Belgium and the United States, both of which had strong economic interests in the Congo. The U.S. and Belgium feared that Lumumba's leftist leanings would lead him to ally with the Soviet Union, and they worked to undermine his government.

Patrice Lumumba

Mobutu Sese Seko.
Source: *themillenium9.wordpress.com/*

The U.S. and Belgium supported rival factions within the Congolese government, including army commander Joseph Mobutu, who eventually launched a coup against Lumumba. Lumumba was captured and handed over to his enemies, who brutally tortured and killed him. His death was a great loss to the Congo and Africa as a whole, underscoring the many challenges that post-colonial nations face in trying to build strong and democratic institutions.

Despite his short time in power, Lumumba's legacy has had a lasting impact on the DRC and on Africa. He was a passionate advocate for democracy and national sovereignty, and his vision of a united, independent Africa continues to inspire activists and leaders across the continent. The brutal manner of his death has also served as a cautionary tale, reminding us of the dangers of outside interference in the affairs of African nations.

Lumumba's death sparked outrage worldwide, with many condemning the brutal manner in which he was killed. It also profoundly impacted the DRC itself, leading to a period of instability and violence. Mobutu, who took power after Lumumba's death, ruled the country for over 30 years, during which time he amassed a fortune while neglecting the needs of his people. The country descended into chaos, with various factions fighting for control, and Mobutu's regime became increasingly authoritarian and corrupt.

However, Lumumba's vision of a united, independent Africa lived on, and his legacy inspired many leaders and activists across the continent. The struggle for democracy and national sovereignty continued, and in the years that followed, many African nations achieved independence from colonial rule. Lumumba's vision of a united Africa also found expression in the Pan-African movement, which sought to promote cooperation and solidarity among African nations.

Today, the legacy of Patrice Lumumba continues to inspire people worldwide. His commitment to democracy, national sovereignty, and pan-Africanism represent a powerful vision of what Africa can be. His tragic death serves as a reminder of the ongoing struggle for self-determination and democratic governance in the face of powerful external forces. While the DRC continues to face many challenges, Lumumba's legacy remains an important source of inspiration for those who seek to build a better future for the country and the continent.

4.3. **MOBUTU SESE SEKO'S DICTATORSHIP**

Mobutu Sese Seko was a Congolese politician who ruled the Democratic Republic of Congo (DRC) for over three decades, from 1965 to 1997. His tenure was marked by authoritarianism, corruption, and economic mismanagement, profoundly impacting the country's political and social landscape.

Mobutu came to power following a coup d'etat in 1965, overthrowing the government of Patrice Lumumba's successor, Joseph Kasavubu. He quickly established himself as an autocratic leader, suppressing political opposition and consolidating power through various means, including using force, propaganda, and patronage.

One of the key features of Mobutu's regime was the creation of a personality cult around himself. He adopted the title of "Sese Seko," which means "the only one who matters," and promoted himself as the father of the nation. He also imposed a strict dress code, "la Sape," which required men to wear suits and ties and banned traditional Congolese dress.

Mobutu's regime was also characterized by corruption and economic mismanagement. He used his position to enrich himself and his supporters while neglecting the country's infrastructure and social services. The country's economy, which had been relatively strong in the early years of his regime, stagnated and eventually collapsed in the 1980s.

Despite these challenges, Mobutu maintained his grip on power for over three decades, thanks in part to the support of Western countries. The United States and other Western powers saw Mobutu as a bulwark against Soviet influence in Africa and provided him with military and economic aid throughout his tenure.

However, Mobutu's rule ended in 1997 following a rebellion led by Laurent-Desire Kabila. Kabila's forces overran the country, and Mobutu fled to exile in Morocco, where he died of cancer in 1997.

In conclusion, the dictatorship of Mobutu Sese Seko had a profound impact on the political and social landscape of the Democratic Republic of Congo. His authoritarianism, corruption, and economic mismanagement contributed to the country's poverty and political instability. While his regime has ended, its legacy continues to be felt in the DRC today, and there is still much work to be done to build a more just and equitable society in the country.

4.4. THE FIRST AND SECOND CONGO WARS

The First Congo War (1996-1997) and the Second Congo War (1998-2003) were two major conflicts that took place in the Democratic Republic of Congo (DRC). The wars were complex and involved multiple parties, with regional and international actors playing a significant role.

The First Congo War began in 1996 when a rebellion led by Laurent-Desire Kabila broke out in the east of the country. Kabila's forces quickly gained control of large parts of the country, including the capital city, Kinshasa. His forces were supported by Rwanda and Uganda, who had their interests in the conflict. Rwanda, in particular, sought to neutralize Hutu militias who fled the DRC after the genocide in Rwanda in 1994.

In May 1997, Kabila declared himself president, and the conflict officially ended. However, Kabila's rule was soon marked by authoritarianism and repression, and tensions began to simmer between him and his former allies, Rwanda and Uganda.

The Second Congo War began in August 1998, when Rwandan and Ugandan forces invaded the DRC, citing security concerns. The conflict quickly escalated, with other regional actors, such as Angola, Zimbabwe, and Namibia, getting involved on the side of the DRC government.

The war was characterized by widespread violence and human rights abuses, with millions killed, displaced, or affected. It was also marked by the widespread exploitation of the DRC's mineral resources, armed groups and foreign companies vying for control of mines and other natural resources.

The Second Congo War ended in 2003, with a peace agreement signed in South Africa. However, the conflict had a lasting impact on the country, with widespread insecurity and political instability continuing today. The conflict also contributed to the ongoing exploitation and underdevelopment of the DRC's natural resources, with many of the country's minerals, such as coltan, used in electronic devices, continuing to be mined under conditions of exploitation and abuse.

4.5. THE KABILA AND KABANGE REGIMES

The Kabila and Kabange regimes in the Democratic Republic of Congo (DRC) have been marked by political instability, human rights abuses, and economic mismanagement. Both regimes have been criticized for their authoritarianism, corruption, and failure to address the country's root causes of conflict and instability.

Laurent-Desire Kabila seized power in 1997 after leading a rebellion against the long-serving dictator Mobutu Sese Seko. Kabila's regime was initially welcomed by many in the country, who saw him as a fresh start after decades of dictatorship. However, Kabila's rule soon became characterized by repression, political violence, and human rights abuses. He was accused of using security forces to silence opposition and dissent and failing to address the economic and social needs of the population.

Laurent Kabila   Joseph Kabila

In 2001, Kabila was assassinated by one of his bodyguards, and his son Joseph Kabila was installed as president. Joseph Kabila's regime continued many of the same practices as his father, with repression of dissent and opposition and little progress on economic and social development. However, his regime made some reforms, including a new constitution in 2006 that aimed to decentralize power and increase democratic participation.

Kabila's rule was marked by several significant events, including the 2006 presidential election, which was widely criticized for its lack of transparency and fairness. Kabila won the election with around 58% of the vote, but opposition candidates and international observers raised concerns about irregularities and fraud.

Kabila's regime also oversaw the controversial 2011 presidential election, in which he was re-elected for a second term. Allegations of vote-rigging and intimidation marred the election, and opposition candidates and civil society groups denounced it as illegitimate.

In 2018, Kabila's regime ended following a presidential election that saw opposition candidate Felix Tshisekedi elected to the presidency. However, Tshisekedi's rule has also been marked by controversy and criticism, with allegations of vote rigging and questions about his legitimacy.

The Kabange regime, led by Prime Minister Augustin Matata Ponyo, took office in 2012 and was tasked with implementing economic reforms and tackling corruption. However, the regime was criticized for its failure to make significant progress on these issues and for continuing to prioritize the interests of the elite over those of the wider population.

Felix Tshisekedi Source *www.bbc.co.uk*

4.6. M23 REBELLION

The M23 rebellion was an armed conflict in the eastern part of the Democratic Republic of Congo from 2012 to 2013. The conflict was fought between the Congolese government forces, supported by United Nations peacekeeping troops, and the M23 rebel group, which was made up of former Congolese soldiers who had defected from the army.

The M23 rebellion was primarily driven by political and economic grievances, including allegations of discrimination against ethnic Tutsis and the Congolese government's failure to implement the terms of a previous peace agreement. The rebel group took control of several towns and villages in the eastern Congo, including the city of Goma, which has more than one million people.

The conflict was characterized by widespread human rights abuses, including killings, rape, and forced displacement of civilians. The UN peacekeeping mission in the Congo (MONUSCO) was heavily involved in the conflict, providing logistical support to the Congolese army and launching offensive operations against the M23 rebels.

The M23 rebellion ended in late 2013 when the rebel group was defeated by Congolese and UN forces. The group's leaders were forced into exile, and several were later arrested and prosecuted for war crimes and crimes against humanity.

The M23 rebellion highlighted several of the underlying issues that have plagued the eastern Congo for decades, including ethnic tensions, political instability, and a lack of effective governance. The conflict was also fueled by exploiting natural resources, particularly coltan, used in electronics production.

The M23 rebellion also had significant regional implications, as neighbouring countries, including Rwanda and Uganda, were accused of supporting the rebel group. Both countries denied the allegations, but the conflict strained diplomatic relations between the Congo and its neighbours.

The M23 rebellion was also a reminder of the challenges facing UN peacekeeping operations in the Congo. MONUSCO, the UN peacekeeping mission in the country, has been present in the Congo since 1999 and is one of the largest UN peacekeeping missions in the world. However, the mission has faced criticism for its effectiveness, particularly in the face of the ongoing conflict in the eastern Congo.

One of the key criticisms of MONUSCO is that it is understaffed and under-resourced, making it difficult for the mission to effectively carry out its mandate to protect civilians and promote peace and stability in the country. The mission has also been criticized for its limited engagement with local communities and its perceived bias in favour of the Congolese government.

The M23 rebellion also highlighted the need for a political solution to the conflict in the Congo. While the defeat of the M23 rebels was a significant military victory, it did not address the underlying political and economic grievances that fueled the conflict. A long-term solution to the conflict will require a comprehensive approach that addresses issues such as governance, security, and economic development.

In recent years, there have been some positive developments in the eastern Congo, including the successful containment of the Ebola outbreak and the establishment of a new government under President Felix Tshisekedi. However, the region remains volatile, with ongoing conflict and human rights abuses perpetrated by various armed groups.

In conclusion, the M23 rebellion was a significant event in the ongoing conflict in the Democratic Republic of Congo. The conflict highlighted the country's challenges, including ethnic tensions, political instability, and the exploitation of natural resources. The conflict also exposed the weaknesses of UN peacekeeping operations in the country and underscored the need for a comprehensive, political solution to the conflict.

5. The Current State of the Democratic Republic of Congo

The Democratic Republic of the Congo (DRC) has a rich and complex history marked by colonization, civil war, and political instability. Despite the end of the Second Congo War in 2003 and establishing a democratic government in 2006, the country still faces significant challenges today. In this section, we will explore the current state of the DRC, examining its political, economic, and social conditions.

5.1. POLITICAL SITUATION

The Democratic Republic of the Congo (DRC) has experienced political turmoil and instability for decades, with its political history marked by coups, rebellions, and power struggles. The country is currently led by President Felix Tshisekedi, who assumed office in January 2019. Allegations of fraud marred his election, but he was eventually declared the winner by the country's electoral commission and confirmed by the Constitutional Court.

Tshisekedi's presidency is notable in that it marks the first time in 18 years that the DRC has had a peaceful power transfer. Tshisekedi's presidency has been marked by efforts to address corruption and improve governance, although progress has been slow. He has also faced challenges in asserting his authority and consolidating power, with Kabila's party, the

People's Party for Reconstruction and Democracy (PPRD), continuing to wield significant influence in the country's political landscape.

The DRC's political scene is characterized by fragmented opposition and the presence of numerous armed groups, some of which are backed by foreign powers. These groups operate in various parts of the country, perpetrating human rights abuses and contributing to the ongoing insecurity in the country. The DRC is also a country with a long history of electoral violence, and concerns remain about the potential for future unrest and instability.

Tshisekedi has sought to address some of these challenges by pursuing dialogue with armed groups and other stakeholders and implementing reforms to improve governance and fight corruption. However, progress in these areas has been slow, and many challenges remain.

Overall, the current political state of the DRC remains fragile and uncertain. The country faces significant challenges in consolidating democracy, improving governance, and addressing the underlying causes of conflict and insecurity. While some progress has been made in recent years, much work remains to be done to ensure a stable and prosperous future for the DRC and its people.

5.2. HUMAN RIGHTS SITUATION

The Democratic Republic of Congo (DRC) has a long history of human rights violations, including extrajudicial killings, rape, forced labour, and other forms of violence. In recent years, the country has faced a new wave of violence, with armed groups operating in various parts of the country, including the east. This has resulted in widespread human rights abuses, including forced displacement of populations, rape, and extrajudicial killings.

The government has been criticized for its response to the violence, with many accusing it of failing to protect its citizens. The government has also been accused of using excessive force against protesters and opposition groups and suppressing freedom of expression and the press.

According to reports, security forces in the DRC have been responsible for numerous human rights violations, including arbitrary arrests, torture, and extrajudicial killings. In addition, the government has been accused of failing to hold perpetrators accountable, leading to a culture of impunity.

The situation for women and children in the DRC is particularly dire, with widespread sexual violence and exploitation reported. Armed groups often target women and girls, and rape is frequently used as a weapon of war.

Human rights violations in the DRC. Source: *https://smallcaps.com.au/*

In addition, the DRC has one of the highest rates of child labour in the world, with children as young as five years old working in mines and other hazardous industries. The country has also been criticized for treating refugees and migrants, with reports of forced deportation and mistreatment.

While the government has taken some steps to address human rights issues, including creating a national human rights commission and signing international human rights treaties, much more needs to be done to protect the rights of citizens in the country.

5.3. ECONOMIC SITUATION

The Democratic Republic of Congo (DRC) is one of the poorest countries in the world despite being rich in natural resources. The country's economy has been plagued by conflict, corruption, and mismanagement, resulting in high poverty levels, unemployment, and underdevelopment.

The DRC's economy heavily depends on extracting natural resources, including copper, cobalt, diamonds, and gold. However, the country's mining industry has been plagued by corruption, with multinational corporations and government officials accused of illegally profiting from the sector.

Despite the country's vast arable land, the DRC's agriculture sector has also been neglected. As a result, the country relies heavily on food imports, leading to high food prices and food insecurity for many citizens.

Furthermore, the country's infrastructure is inadequate, with poor road networks, unreliable electricity supply, and limited access to clean water and sanitation facilities. This has led to significant challenges for businesses and hindered economic growth.

In recent years, the DRC's economy has been impacted by the COVID-19 pandemic, with reduced demand for its natural resources and disruptions to supply chains. The pandemic has also exacerbated existing economic challenges, including high levels of debt and inflation.

Despite these challenges, the DRC has improved its economic situation. The government has launched initiatives to attract foreign investment, including tax incentives and streamlined business setting procedures. The country has also secured debt relief from international organizations, which has helped to reduce its debt burden.

However, much more must be done to address the root causes of the DRC's economic challenges. This includes tackling corruption, improving infrastructure, and diversifying the economy beyond the extractive industries. The government must also prioritize the development of the agriculture sector to improve food security and reduce dependence on imports.

5.4. SECURITY SITUATION

The Democratic Republic of the Congo (DRC) has faced a complex and multifaceted security situation for several decades. The country has experienced prolonged conflict, political instability, and violence that has displaced millions of people, caused loss of life and destruction of infrastructure. Several factors, including ethnic tensions, competition for resources, and the presence of various armed groups, have fueled the ongoing security crisis in the DRC.

Soldiers in the DRC. Image credit: MONUSCO Photos.

One of the most significant security challenges facing the DRC is the presence of various armed groups, some of which have been operating in the country for decades. These armed groups have been involved in numerous human rights violations, including recruiting child soldiers, sexual violence against women and girls, and the displacement of entire communities. The most notorious of these groups is the Allied Democratic Forces (ADF), a Ugandan rebel group operating in the eastern DRC since the 1990s. The ADF has been responsible for numerous attacks on civilians, including massacres and kidnappings, and is believed to be responsible for the deaths of thousands of people.

The DRC's security situation is further complicated by other armed groups, including local militias, rebel groups, and foreign mercenaries. These groups are often involved in illegal resource extraction, including gold, diamonds, and coltan, contributing to the country's ongoing conflict and instability. In addition, the lack of effective governance and law enforcement has allowed criminal networks to thrive, leading to increased levels of violent crime and insecurity.

Another major security challenge facing the DRC is the on-going inter-communal conflict, particularly in the country's eastern regions. Ethnic and territorial tensions largely drive the conflict and has displaced millions of people. The government has attempted to address the issue through various initiatives, including disarmament and reintegration programs, but these efforts have largely been ineffective.

The DRC's security situation has also been impacted by the COVID-19 pandemic, which has put additional strain on the country's already fragile healthcare system and economy. The pandemic has significantly reduced revenue from exports, leading to a further decline in the country's already struggling economy.

6. Importance of the Democratic Republic of the Congo in the Global Economy

Strategic location: The DRC is located in the heart of Africa and is bordered by nine countries. This strategic location has made it a hub for trade and commerce and a key player in regional politics.

The Democratic Republic of Congo (DRC) is the second-largest country in Africa by land area and the 11th-largest globally. The country is strategically located in the centre of the African continent. It has a vast network of rivers and access to the Atlantic Ocean, making it an important country for Africa and the world.

Firstly, DRC's location in the heart of Africa gives it immense importance as a gateway to the continent. The country shares borders with nine other African countries, making it a hub for trade and commerce. Its location also makes it an important transit point for goods and people travelling across the continent. The country's vast network of rivers, including the Congo River, the second-longest river in Africa, makes it an important transportation hub for goods and people.

Secondly, DRC's strategic location also makes it an important country for natural resources. The country has vast mineral resources, including cobalt, copper, gold, and diamonds, crucial for global electronics, construction, and automotive industries. The DRC is also home to the largest rainforest in Africa, the

Congo Basin, which plays a vital role in regulating the Earth's climate and is home to numerous endangered species.

Thirdly, the DRC's location also gives it geopolitical importance. The country's position in the heart of Africa has made it a battleground for regional and international powers seeking to exert influence over the continent. Throughout its history, the DRC has been embroiled in numerous conflicts involving neighbouring countries and international actors. The country's location has made it a focal point for regional integration efforts, such as the Southern African Development Community (SADC) and the Economic Community of Central African States (ECCAS).

Lastly, DRC's strategic location also gives it an important role in promoting peace and stability in the region. The country's vast size and natural resources have made it a source of conflict, with numerous rebel groups vying for control over mineral resources. However, the country's strategic location has also made it a key player in regional peacekeeping efforts, with the United Nations maintaining a large peacekeeping force since 1999.

Abundant natural resources: The DRC is one of the world's richest countries in terms of natural resources. One of the most significant contributions of the DRC to the global economy is the mining sector. The country is a leading producer of copper and cobalt, critical minerals for producing batteries used in electric vehicles, renewable energy systems, and mobile phones. For instance, the DRC accounts for approximately 60% of the global cobalt supply, making the country an essential player in the global transition to green energy.

Mining in DRC

The DRC also has significant reserves of other minerals, including gold, tin, tantalum, and tungsten, essential for producing various consumer goods such as electronics, jewellery, and automobiles. The DRC's mineral resources are strategically important to many countries, including China, the United States, and the European Union.

The Democratic Republic of Congo (DRC) is a country known for its abundant natural resources, which are of great importance to Africa and the world.

Firstly, the DRC is known for its vast mineral resources, including copper, cobalt, diamonds, and gold. These minerals are essential for producing various industrial and technological products, such as smartphones, electric cars, and renewable energy technologies. The DRC's mineral wealth significantly affects the global economy, as it contributes to producing these essential goods and services.

Secondly, the DRC's natural resources are of great importance to the African continent, as they have the potential to drive economic growth and development. The country's mineral wealth provides opportunities for job creation, foreign investment, and revenue generation for the government. Moreover, the DRC's natural resources can contribute to the development of other African countries through regional trade and investment.

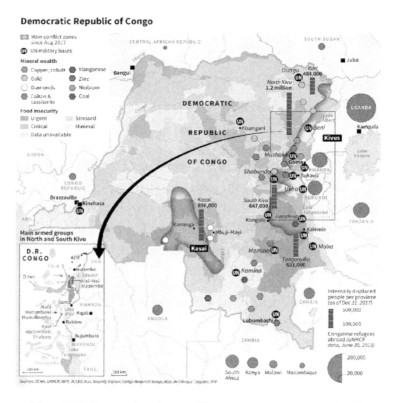

Map of DR Congo, showing conflict zones, Source Image Credit

Thirdly, the exploitation of the DRC's natural resources has significantly impacted the environment and the local communities. The mining industry has been associated with environmental degradation, deforestation, and pollution, which negatively affect the health and livelihoods of local communities. Moreover, the extraction of natural resources has been linked to human rights abuses, including forced labour and child labour.

Fourthly, the DRC's natural resources have also been a source of conflict and political instability. The country's mineral wealth has attracted international competition and geopolitical rivalries, contributing to the ongoing conflict and violence in the region. Exploiting natural resources has also been a driver of corruption and illegal trade, undermining governance and the rule of law.

Lastly, the DRC's natural resources can be a source of cooperation and integration, both regionally and globally. The country is a member of the African Union and has participated in regional initiatives such as the African Mining Vision, which aims to promote sustainable and responsible mining practices on the continent. The DRC's engagement in such initiatives can contribute to developing African unity and cooperation, which can have far-reaching implications for the continent's growth and future.

Environmental significance: The DRC is home to the Congo Basin, the world's second-largest rainforest. This rainforest is a critical carbon sink, which helps mitigate climate change by absorbing carbon dioxide from the atmosphere.

The country has vast forest resources, which make it a significant supplier of wood products to countries in Europe, Asia, and the Americas. The timber industry is a major employer in the country, providing jobs for thousands of people.

The Democratic Republic of Congo (DRC) is a country of immense environmental significance to Africa and the world. The country is home to the largest rainforest in Africa, the Congo Basin, which plays a vital role in regulating the Earth's climate and is home to numerous endangered species. Below is the importance of the DRC's environmental significance to Africa and the world.

Firstly, the Congo Basin rainforest is one of the most biologically diverse regions on the planet, with an estimated 10,000 plant species and over 400 mammal species. The forest also supports numerous endangered species, including forest elephants, gorillas, chimpanzees, and bonobos. These species are important for their intrinsic value and have cultural and economic significance for the local communities that depend on them for their livelihoods.

Africa S Rainforests Are Different Why It Matters That They Re Protected from
images.theconversation.com

The Congo Basin Rainforest shares many characteristics with the Amazon rainforest and other tropical forests worldwide: The two forests are on the same latitude and contain mostly the same plants and animals. It is a collection of forests, rivers, swamps and savannas. The forests of the congo basin are characterized by fewer species of trees than the Amazon rainforest. It's also responsible for 40% of the world's oxygen. The congo basin forest, the second largest in the world after the amazon, has been relatively protected by its inaccessibility

Secondly, the Congo Basin is vital in regulating the Earth's climate. The rainforest absorbs vast amounts of carbon dioxide, which helps reduce climate change's impact. The Congo Basin is estimated to store approximately 25% of the world's tropical forest carbon, making it an important carbon sink. Deforestation, however, threatens this crucial rainforest function and could have severe global consequences.

Thirdly, the DRC's environmental significance extends beyond the Congo Basin rainforest. The country is also home to numerous other important ecosystems, including wetlands, savannas, and mountains. These ecosystems provide important ecological services, such as water filtration, erosion control, and carbon sequestration, and support local communities that depend on them for their livelihoods.

Lastly, the DRC's environmental significance also has economic and political implications. The country's vast natural resources, including timber and minerals, have been a source of conflict and exploitation. The government and international actors have worked to promote sustainable development and conservation efforts in the country, but much work remains to be done.

Humanitarian crisis: The DRC has been plagued by ongoing conflicts and humanitarian crises for decades. The country has one of the world's highest levels of internal displacement, with millions of people forced to flee their homes due to conflict and insecurity. The crisis has had a significant impact on Africa and the world, and below, we will explore the importance of the DRC's humanitarian crisis.

Firstly, the DRC's humanitarian crisis has had a devastating impact on the people of the country. Millions of people have been forced to flee their homes due to conflict and violence, and many have been subjected to human rights abuses, including sexual violence and forced labour. The crisis has resulted in widespread poverty and malnutrition, with many people lacking access to basic services such as healthcare and education. This humanitarian crisis has profoundly impacted the country's development and future prospects.

Secondly, the DRC's humanitarian crisis has significantly impacted the African continent's stability. The ongoing conflict in the country has spilt over into neighbouring countries, leading to further instability and conflict. The influx of refugees into neighbouring countries has also put pressure on already fragile economies and strained resources. The instability and conflict in the DRC have a ripple effect throughout the region, with implications for the wider African continent.

Thirdly, the DRC's humanitarian crisis has global implications. The conflict and displacement in the country have contributed to the global refugee crisis, with millions of people forced to flee their homes in search of safety. This crisis has put pressure on countries worldwide to provide assistance and support to refugees. Additionally, the conflict in the DRC has been fueled by exploiting the country's natural resources, including minerals used in producing electronics and other products. Exploiting these resources has led to environmental degradation and human rights abuses, with implications for consumers worldwide.

Lastly, the DRC's humanitarian crisis has political and security implications. The ongoing conflict in the country has created a power vacuum that has allowed armed groups to thrive, perpetuating the cycle of violence and instability. The international community has struggled to address the crisis, with efforts to promote peace and stability often hampered by political and economic interests.

In conclusion, the instability and conflict in the DRC have also had implications for the stability of the African continent and beyond, contributing to the global refugee crisis and fueling environmental degradation and human rights abuses. Addressing the crisis will require a concerted effort by the international community to promote peace, stability, and development in the country

Political influence: The DRC is a major player in African politics, with a population of over 100 million people and a strategic location in the continent's heart. The country's political leadership significantly influences the African Union and other regional organizations.

The Democratic Republic of Congo (DRC) is a country that holds significant political influence not only in Africa but also in the world as a whole.

Firstly, the DRC is Africa's second-largest country, with over 100 million people. As such, it is a significant player in African politics, and its decisions and actions can profoundly impact the continent. The country's strategic location, rich natural resources, and size make it an influential player in regional politics.

Secondly, the DRC has a complex political history with a legacy of authoritarian rule, corruption, and conflict. The country has experienced multiple coups, civil wars, and political crises, contributing to its instability and fragility. The political situation in the DRC has implications for the wider African continent, as it can destabilize neighbouring countries and create a ripple effect throughout the region.

Thirdly, the DRC's political influence extends beyond Africa, as the country is rich in natural resources such as copper, cobalt, and diamonds, which are highly sought after in the global economy. Exploiting these resources has led to geopolitical competition between international players, including China, the US, and the EU. The DRC's political decisions regarding managing its natural resources have global implications for the economy, environment, and human rights.

Fourthly, the DRC's political influence is also felt in the international arena, as the country is a member of the United Nations and has a voice in global decision-making. The DRC's position on climate change, human rights, and conflict resolution can significantly impact global policy and action.

Lastly, the DRC's political influence is significant regarding its potential to promote regional integration and cooperation. The country is a member of the African Union and has participated in regional initiatives such as the Great Lakes Pact, which aims to promote peace, stability, and development in the region. The DRC's engagement in such initiatives can advance African unity and cooperation, which can have far-reaching implications for the continent's development and future.

Given these factors, the DRC has significant importance both for Africa and the world. Its abundant natural resources have made it a key player in global markets, while it's strategic location and political influence has made it a critical player in African politics. At the same time, the country's ongoing humanitarian crisis underscores the need for greater attention and investment in the country's development and stability. As such, the DRC is a complex and multifaceted country that is of critical importance to the world as a whole.

Furthermore, the DRC's economic potential and natural resources are crucial for the development and stability of the African continent. The country's rich mineral resources, including cobalt, copper, and diamonds, are essential for producing modern technologies and infrastructure necessary for economic growth and development. The DRC's hydropower potential is also significant, with the Inga Dam on the Congo River having the potential to generate 40,000 megawatts of electricity, making it one of the world's largest hydroelectric power stations.

In addition to its economic and environmental significance, the DRC is important for Africa's peace and security. The country's ongoing conflicts and humanitarian crises have had a spillover effect in the region, with refugees fleeing to neighbouring countries and instability spreading beyond its borders. The UN peacekeeping mission in the DRC, known as MONUSCO, is the largest UN peacekeeping mission in the world, highlighting the importance of the country's stability to regional security.

The DRC's importance also extends beyond Africa, as it is a major source of raw materials for global markets, including for industries such as technology, automotive, and construction. The country's natural resources and economic potential have attracted significant foreign investment, with China, the European Union, and the United States among the largest investors in the country.

In conclusion, the Democratic Republic of the Congo is immensely important for Africa and the world. Its strategic location, abundant natural resources, environmental significance, political influence, and ongoing humanitarian crisis make it a complex and multifaceted country. The country's economic potential and natural resources are crucial for the development and stability of the African continent. At the same time, its importance for peace and security underscores the need for greater attention and investment in its development.

6.1. DRC'S MINERAL RESOURCES

The Democratic Republic of the Congo is home to abundant mineral resources that play a significant role in the global economy. The Democratic Republic of Congo (DRC) is rich in natural resources, with an estimated $24 trillion worth of untapped mineral reserves, including cobalt, copper, and diamonds. These resources have played a significant role in shaping the global economy, as they are essential for various industries, including technology and renewable energy.

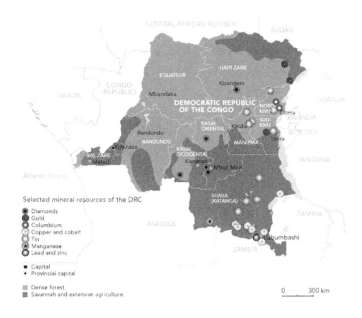

Selected Minerals in DRC *www.bbc.co.uk*

The country is estimated to possess 70% of the world's coltan reserves, a vital mineral used in producing electronic devices such as smartphones, laptops, and gaming consoles. It also has the world's largest cobalt reserves, an essential component in rechargeable batteries used in electric cars, aerospace, and defence industries. The global demand for electric vehicles has increased, leading to a surge in demand for cobalt. This demand has resulted in a sharp rise in the price of cobalt, which has benefited the DRC's economy. In 2018, the DRC earned over $1.2 billion from cobalt exports alone.

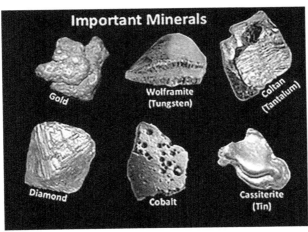

Minerals from DRC mines. Source *https://www.sputtertargets.net/*

One of the most valuable resources in the DRC is cobalt, which is used to produce rechargeable batteries for electric vehicles and other electronics. The country is responsible for more than 60% of global cobalt production, making it a critical player in the global market. However, the cobalt industry in the DRC is plagued by issues such as child labour and dangerous working conditions, with many small-scale miners working in unsafe and unregulated mines.

Electric vehicle *www.fool.com*

Coltan or Columbine-tantalite is one of the minerals mined in the Democratic Republic of the Congo by slave labour controlled by armed factions. It is the mineral used to produce Tantalum, a highly corrosion-resistant metal widely used in capacitors of electronic products like cell phones, DVD players, video game systems and computers. The cell phone you're using right now (or that PC you're reading this book on) could very well contain Tantalum from coltan mined in the Congo.

The DRC is also home to significant copper reserves, which are vital in producing electrical wiring and other electronics. The country is responsible for around 5% of global copper production, with the mining industry being dominated by foreign companies such as Glencore and China Molybdenum.

Diamond mining is another critical sector in the DRC's economy. The country is among the world's top ten producers of diamonds, with most of the production coming from the Kasai region. The diamond industry provides significant revenues for the country, and it is estimated that diamonds account for approximately 10% of the country's exports. The country is Africa's largest producer of industrial diamonds and the third-largest globally. The diamond industry has played a significant role in the country's history, particularly during the colonial era when forced labour was used to extract diamonds. Today, the diamond industry is regulated by the government and has been subject to international scrutiny to prevent the trade of conflict diamonds, also known as blood diamonds.

However, despite abundant mineral resources in the DRC, the country has not benefited significantly from its mining sector. The sector has been plagued by corruption, mismanagement, and conflicts, leading to the exploitation of the country's resources by foreign companies and illegal armed groups. This has resulted in minimal economic development, little infrastructure, and widespread poverty in the country.

In recent years, there have been efforts to address these issues and reform the mining sector. The government has introduced new mining laws to increase transparency, improve governance, and increase revenues for the country. The DRC has also joined the Extractive Industries Transparency Initiative (EITI), which requires companies to disclose their payments to governments, and the government to disclose its revenues from the mining sector.

The importance of the DRC's mineral resources in the global economy cannot be overstated. The demand for these resources is increasing, driven by the growth of the electronics, automotive, and renewable energy industries. As the DRC continues to reform its mining sector and improve governance, it can become a significant player in the global economy and provide significant revenues for its development.

The global reliance on the DRC's resources has positive and negative effects on the country's economy. On the one hand, it provides significant revenue to the government, which can be used to fund development projects and improve the standard of living for the population. On the other hand, the extraction of these resources has led to environmental degradation, social and political instability, and the exploitation of workers. Additionally, the overreliance on these resources has made the DRC's economy vulnerable to fluctuations in global commodity prices.

Given the importance of these resources, it is not surprising that the global economy is heavily reliant on the DRC. According to the World Bank, the DRC is the world's leading producer of cobalt, and it is estimated to hold around 50% of the world's reserves. It is also one of the largest producers of copper and diamonds globally. In 2020, the DRC was the world's eighth-largest producer of copper, with an output of around 1.5 million tonnes. The country is also estimated to hold approximately 10% of the world's diamonds.

NATURAL RESOURCES
A world of minerals in your mobile phone
More than half of a mobile phone's components - including its electronics, display, battery and speakers - are made from mined and semi-processed materials.

In addition to minerals, the DRC also has significant timber reserves, a valuable export product. However, the logging industry in the country is also characterized by corruption and unsustainable practices, with illegal logging and poor regulation contributing to deforestation and environmental degradation.

The DRC also has significant agricultural potential, with fertile land and a favourable climate for coffee, cocoa, and palm oil crops. However, the agriculture sector in the country is underdeveloped, with poor infrastructure, limited investment, and low productivity hindering its potential.

The DRC's importance in the global economy is evident in the significant foreign investment it attracts. The country has recently witnessed a surge in foreign investment, particularly in the mining sector. The Chinese have been particularly active in investing in the DRC, with Chinese companies owning significant stakes in many mining operations. The United States and European countries also have a considerable presence in the country's mining sector.

However, despite its abundance of mineral resources, the DRC remains one of the world's poorest countries, with a gross domestic product (GDP) per capita of around $496 in 2019. This disparity is due to corruption, poor governance, and conflict. The country has also been struggling with the effects of the COVID-19 pandemic, which has adversely affected its economy.

In conclusion, the DRC's mineral resources are critical to the global economy. The country is a significant producer of cobalt, copper, and diamonds, which are essential for various industries, including technology and renewable energy. The world's reliance on these resources is evident in the significant foreign investment the DRC attracts, particularly in the mining sector. However, despite its mineral wealth, the country remains one of the world's poorest, indicating the need for more significant efforts to ensure its resources benefit the local population.

6.2. THE IMPACT OF RESOURCE EXTRACTION IN THE DRC

The Democratic Republic of Congo (DRC) is a country rich in natural resources, including minerals such as cobalt, copper, diamonds, timber, and fertile agricultural land. However, exploiting these resources has significantly impacted the country's economy and politics, contributing to a cycle of corruption, conflict, and poverty.

Resource extraction has been a significant driver of the DRC's economy, accounting for around 95% of the country's exports. The mining industry, in particular, has significantly contributed to the country's GDP, with copper and cobalt being the most valuable exports. However, the benefits of this industry have been largely concentrated in the hands of a small elite, with the majority of the population seeing little or no benefit.

The mining industry in the DRC has been characterized by corruption, with foreign companies often colluding with government officials to secure favourable contracts and avoid taxes. This has led to a situation where the majority of the wealth generated by the industry is siphoned off by foreign companies and corrupt officials rather than being used to benefit the population.

The impact of resource extraction on the DRC's politics has also been significant. The country has a long history of conflict and instability, with various armed groups and militias vying to control valuable resources. This has contributed to a cycle of violence and exploitation, with civilians often bearing the brunt of the conflict and suffering from human rights abuses.

The exploitation of resources has also significantly impacted the environment, with mining and logging contributing to deforestation and environmental degradation. This has significantly impacted the country's indigenous populations, who rely on the forest for their livelihoods.

In addition to the negative impact on the environment and local communities, the concentration of wealth in the hands of a small elite has also significantly impacted the country's economy. The lack of investment in infrastructure and other sectors of the economy has left the country heavily dependent on resource extraction with little diversification.

The impact of resource extraction on the DRC's economy and politics has been significant, contributing to a cycle of poverty, conflict, and corruption. Addressing these issues will require significant reform, including greater transparency in the mining industry, increased investment in infrastructure and other sectors of the economy, and a focus on sustainable development and equitable distribution of wealth. Only through such measures can the DRC begin to unlock the full potential of its natural resources and ensure a brighter future for its citizens.

6.3. THE ROLE OF MULTINATIONAL CORPORATIONS IN DRC

The exploitation of the Democratic Republic of Congo's (DRC) natural resources by multinational corporations and foreign governments has been a major factor in the country's ongoing conflicts and economic challenges. These resources, which include minerals such as cobalt, copper, and coltan, are vital components of many high-tech products such as smartphones, electric cars, and laptops.

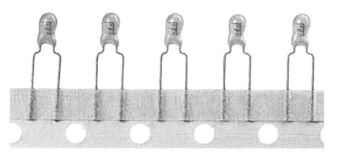

Tantallum Source *https://www.sputtertargets.net/*

Foreign companies have long been mining these resources, often with little regard for the impact on local communities or the environment. The history of foreign exploitation of the DRC's natural resources can be traced back to the colonial era when Belgium's King Leopold II claimed the country as his personal property and used forced labour to extract rubber and other resources.

In recent years, multinational corporations have played a major role in exploiting the DRC's resources. These companies have often been accused of engaging in corrupt practices and exploiting loopholes in the country's weak regulatory framework to maximize profits at the expense of local communities.

One example of such exploitation is the cobalt industry, which foreign corporations dominate. Cobalt is a key component in the batteries that power many electronic devices, and the DRC is the world's largest mineral producer. However, the industry has been plagued by allegations of child labour, poor working conditions, environmental degradation, and human rights abuses.

Another example is the mining of coltan, which is used in producing tantalum capacitors in electronic devices. Foreign companies have been accused of fueling conflict in the eastern DRC by buying coltan from armed groups and militias, who use the profits to finance their activities.

Foreign governments have also exploited the DRC's resources, often by supporting corrupt regimes and engaging in neocolonial practices. For example, during the Cold War, the United States and other Western powers supported the regime of Mobutu Sese Seko, despite widespread corruption and human rights abuses. Mobutu allowed foreign corporations to exploit the country's resources with little oversight while diverting much of the profits to his personal accounts.

China has also recently become a major player in the DRC's mining sector, often through state-owned enterprises. While China has promised to invest in infrastructure and development projects in exchange for access to the DRC's resources, there are concerns that this investment may be driven more by a desire for strategic control over critical minerals than by a genuine commitment to development.

Here are some examples of exploitation of Congolese by Multinational Corporation

Mineral exploitation: The DRC is home to a wide range of minerals, including cobalt, copper, and coltan, essential for electronics production. Multinational corporations worldwide have been eager to extract these minerals, often through deals with the government that are not transparent and do not benefit the local population. This has led to environmental degradation and human rights abuses, such as forced and child labour.

Timber exploitation: The DRC is home to some of the world's largest tropical forests, which are a valuable source of timber. However, illegal logging and poor management of these forests have led to deforestation, harming the environment and impacting the livelihoods of the people who depend on the forests.

Land grabbing: Foreign governments and corporations have also been accused of taking land from the Congolese people for their purposes, such as constructing mines or large-scale agricultural projects. This has often been done without the consent of the local population and has led to displacement and the loss of traditional livelihoods.

Exploiting these resources has had a significant impact on the economy and politics of the DRC. While the country is rich in natural resources, the profits from their exploitation have not been used to benefit the Congolese people. Instead, they have often been siphoned off by corrupt officials or foreign companies, leaving the country with little to show for its vast resources.

Furthermore, the reliance on resource extraction has created a boom-and-bust cycle in the DRC's economy, with the country's fortunes rising and falling with global commodity prices. This has led to a lack of economic diversification, which makes the country vulnerable to external shocks and leaves the population vulnerable to poverty and instability.

Resource Conflict — The conflict has involved various armed groups, foreign governments, multinational corporations, and local communities seeking control of these resources. During the First Congo War (1996-1997), the primary driver of the conflict was the desire to control the resources of the eastern part of the country, especially in the Kivu and Ituri regions. The

Rwandan government, which backed the rebel group led by Laurent Kabila, sought to control these resources, as they were vital to Rwanda's economic development. The rebel group, known as the Alliance of Democratic Forces for the Liberation of Congo (ADFL), captured the key towns of Goma and Bukavu in 1996, and by May 1997, they had taken control of the capital city, Kinshasa and declared Kabila as the new president.

During the second Congo War, the primary driver of the conflict was still the control of natural resources, especially in the eastern part of the country. Rebel groups such as the Congolese Rally for Democracy (RCD) and the Movement for the Liberation of Congo (MLC) fought to control these resources, with support from Rwanda and Uganda, respectively. The conflict resulted in the deaths of over five million people, with many of these deaths due to disease and hunger resulting from the war.

Multinational corporations have also played a significant role in fueling the conflict. Companies such as AngloGold Ashanti, Barrick Gold, and Glencore have been accused of supporting armed groups and exploiting resources in the eastern part of the country. These companies have been criticized for lacking transparency in their operations and failing to adhere to human rights standards. The United Nations has also accused some multinational corporations of profiting from the conflict by purchasing minerals from armed groups, providing them with the funds to continue their activities.

Foreign governments have also been implicated in fueling the conflict. Rwanda and Uganda, in particular, have been accused of backing rebel groups and exploiting resources in the eastern part of the country. The United Nations has accused both countries of violating the arms embargo and supporting armed groups in the DRC. In 2005, the International Court of Justice ruled that Uganda had violated international law by invading the DRC in 1998 and 1999.

A recent report by the UN calls for financial restrictions to be levied on 54 individuals and 29 companies who are involved in the plunder of DCR, including four Belgian diamond companies and the Belgian company George Forrest, which is partnered with the US-based OM Group. The report also accused 85 South African, European and US multinational corporations — including Anglo-American, Barclays Bank, Bayer, De Beers and the Cabot Corporation — of violating the Organisation for Economic Cooperation and Development's (OECD) ethical guidelines on conflict zones.

'Despite the recent withdrawal of most foreign forces, the exploitation of Congo's resources continues, the report says, with elite networks and criminal groups tied to the military forces of Rwanda, Uganda and Zimbabwe benefiting from micro-conflicts in the D.R.C. "The elite networks derive financial benefit through various criminal activities, including theft, embezzlement, diversion of public funds, undervaluation of goods, smuggling, false invoicing, non-payment of taxes and bribery.' And so, while millions die in Africa with the collaboration of these corporations, European and North American citizens enjoy electric vehicles (containing cobalt) and electronic devices (containing tantalum, tin and gold).

The conflict over resources has also significantly impacted the local communities in the DRC. Many communities have been displaced from their homes, and their livelihoods have been destroyed due to the activities of armed groups and multinational corporations. The conflict has also resulted in the loss of cultural heritage, with the destruction of historical sites and the looting of artefacts.

In conclusion, the conflict over natural resources has been a significant driver of violence and instability in the DRC. The desire to control these resources has fueled the First and Second Congo Wars, and armed groups, foreign governments, and multinational corporations have all exploited these resources. The conflict has resulted in the deaths of millions of people and has had a devastating impact on local communities. Addressing the root causes of the conflict and ensuring that natural resources are managed transparently and sustainably will be essential to achieving lasting peace

6.4. THE CHALLENGES FACING THE DEMOCRATIC REPUBLIC OF THE CONGO

Political challenges — The Democratic Republic of the Congo (DRC) has faced significant political challenges since gaining independence from Belgium in 1960. The country has experienced dictatorship, civil wars, and economic struggles. Although the country has made progress in recent years, it still faces several political challenges.

Weak Institutions and Governance — The DRC's political institutions and governance structures are weak and ineffective. Corruption, mismanagement, and political interference have hampered the government's ability to provide essential services and implement meaningful reforms. The country ranks among the world's most corrupt, affecting its ability to attract foreign investment and promote economic growth.

Ethnic and Regional Tensions — The DRC is home to more than 250 ethnic groups, each with its culture, language, and traditions. This diversity has often been a source of conflict and tension, leading to violence and political instability. Ethnic and regional groups have frequently been pitted against each other, with political elites using these divisions to gain and maintain power.

Electoral Challenges — Irregularities, voter fraud, and violence have plagued the DRC's electoral process. Elections have often been marred by violence and have not been free and fair, leading to a lack of trust in the electoral system. The country's opposition parties have frequently accused the government of rigging elections to remain in power, leading to protests and unrest.

Security Challenges — The DRC has struggled with security challenges for decades, with various rebel groups operating in the eastern part of the country. These groups have been responsible for widespread human rights abuses, including rape, murder, and forced displacement. The Congolese military and the United Nations peacekeeping mission have struggled to contain these groups, leading to ongoing insecurity and instability.

International Intervention — The DRC's political challenges have drawn significant international attention, with various countries and international organizations providing assistance and intervention. While this intervention has helped address some of the country's challenges, it has also led to accusations of foreign interference and a lack of ownership over the country's political and economic development.

Economic challenges — The Democratic Republic of the Congo (DRC) is a country rich in natural resources, yet it remains one of the poorest countries in the world. The DRC has faced significant economic challenges throughout its history, with the exploitation of its natural resources by foreign entities being a major contributing factor. Today, the country faces a range of economic challenges that continue to hinder its development.

Lack of Infrastructure — One of the main challenges facing the DRC is the lack of infrastructure. The country's road, rail, and air networks are poorly developed, making transportation difficult and expensive. This lack of infrastructure also hinders the development of the country's agriculture sector, which is largely dependent on subsistence farming. The lack of infrastructure also makes it difficult for the country to attract foreign investment. Investors are often deterred by the high transportation costs and difficulty getting goods to market.

Corruption — Corruption is widespread in the country, with many officials using their positions of power to enrich themselves at the expense of the population. Corruption is also a major hindrance to foreign investment, as investors are wary of putting their money into a country where corruption is rampant.

Debt burden.- The country owes billions of dollars to foreign creditors, including the International Monetary Fund (IMF) and the World Bank. This debt burden is a major hindrance to the country's development, as it limits the amount of money that the government can spend on social services and infrastructure.

In addition to these challenges, the DRC also faces several other economic problems, including high unemployment, inflation, and poverty. The country's economy is largely dependent on the export of natural resources, particularly copper and cobalt, which makes it vulnerable to fluctuations in global commodity prices.

To address these challenges, the DRC government has taken a number of steps, including implementing economic reforms and working to attract foreign investment. The government has also worked to improve the country's infrastructure, with plans to build new roads, railways, and airports. However, progress has been slow, and much work remains to be done to overcome the DRC's economic challenges.

6.5. THE ENVIRONMENTAL IMPACTS OF THE DEMOCRATIC REPUBLIC OF THE CONGO

The Democratic Republic of the Congo (DRC) is known for its rich natural resources, including vast forests and diverse wildlife. However, the country's environment is facing significant challenges due to decades of deforestation, mining, and other human activities. This section will examine the environmental impact of the DRC and the potential consequences for both the country and the world.

Deforestation — Deforestation is one of the DRC's most significant environmental challenges. The country's rainforest is the second-largest in the world after the Amazon and is home to various plant and animal species. However, deforestation rates in the DRC have been alarmingly high in recent years, with estimates suggesting that the country lost 1.6 million hectares of forest each year between 2000 and 2010.

The primary driver of deforestation in the DRC is commercial agriculture, particularly the production of palm oil and soybeans. Small-scale agriculture, logging, and fuelwood collection also contribute to deforestation. Deforestation has a range of negative impacts, including soil erosion, loss of biodiversity, and increased carbon emissions.

Mining — The DRC is also home to vast mineral resources, including copper, cobalt, and diamonds. However, mining activities in the country have had a significant environmental impact. The extraction of minerals requires clearing forests and excavating soil, leading to soil erosion and water pollution. Additionally, the mining industry is a significant contributor to greenhouse gas emissions.

The mining industry in the DRC has also been linked to human rights abuses, with reports of forced labour, child labour, and other forms of exploitation. The lack of regulation in the industry has allowed mining companies to operate without sufficient oversight, leading to environmental and social harm.

Wildlife Conservation — The DRC is home to some of the most diverse wildlife in the world, including gorillas, elephants, and hippos. However, wildlife populations in the country have been severely impacted by habitat loss, hunting, and poaching. The destruction of forests for agriculture and mining has reduced the habitat available for wildlife, while hunting and poaching have decimated populations of some species.

A lack of resources and political instability have hindered conservation efforts in the DRC. The country's ongoing conflicts have made it challenging to establish protected areas and enforce regulations against poaching and wildlife trafficking.

Consequences of Inaction — The environmental challenges facing the DRC have significant consequences for both the country and the world. Deforestation and mining activities can potentially cause long-term damage to the country's ecosystems, reducing biodiversity and contributing to climate change. The loss of wildlife populations could have significant ecological impacts, affecting the health and functioning of entire ecosystems.

In addition to environmental consequences, inaction on these issues could have social and economic consequences for the DRC. The country's reliance on natural resources for its economy means that environmental degradation could impact the livelihoods of millions of people. Additionally, mining activities and deforestation's social and environmental impacts could lead to increased social unrest and instability.

In conclusion, the DRC's environmental challenges are significant and require urgent attention. The government and international community must work together to address these issues, including implementing measures to protect forests, regulate mining activities, and conserve wildlife. Failure to act could devastate the country's environment, economy, and people.

7. Prospects for Democracy in the Democratic Republic of the Congo

The Democratic Republic of the Congo (DRC) has a long and tumultuous history of political instability, authoritarian rule, and conflict. However, recent efforts have been towards democratization, including the 2006 Constitution establishing a multi-party democratic system and the peaceful transfer of power in 2019. Despite these developments, there are still challenges and obstacles to achieving true democracy in the DRC.

The lack of institutional capacity and effective governance.- Corruption, nepotism, and the weak rule of law have undermined democratic institutions and impeded progress towards democratization. The government's ability to provide basic services, maintain security, and enforce the law is often limited. This has led to popular disillusionment with democracy and a sense of frustration among citizens who feel that democratic institutions have failed them.

The legacy of authoritarianism and political violence. The long history of dictatorship, civil wars, and human rights abuses has created a culture of fear and mistrust that is difficult to overcome. Many political actors, including those in the current government, have been implicated in human rights violations, corruption, and other abuses. This makes it difficult to build trust in democratic institutions and ensure accountability.

The influence of external actors on the political landscape.
— International powers, including neighbouring countries and
multinational corporations, have often shaped political out-
comes in the DRC. This has led to a situation where the interests of foreign actors often precede the Congolese people's
needs and desires. Foreign troops, economic exploitation, and
interference in domestic politics have fueled conflict and undermined democracy.

Despite these challenges, there are some reasons for optimism
regarding the prospects for democracy in the DRC. Civil society and political activists have shown a strong commitment to
democratic values and have pushed for greater accountability
and transparency in government. There has also been progress
towards decentralization, with new provinces and devolving of
some powers to local governments.

The role of international actors in supporting democratization
efforts in the DRC will be crucial. This includes assisting institutional capacity building, supporting civil society, and promoting transparency and accountability. International pressure and engagement can also encourage the government to
respect human rights and ensure democratic processes.

In conclusion, the prospects for democracy in the DRC are
mixed. Challenges and obstacles to achieving true democratization include weak institutions, political violence, and external interference. However, there are also reasons for optimism,
including a commitment to democratic values among civil society and political activists and progress towards decentralization. The role of international actors in supporting democratization efforts will be crucial in overcoming these challenges
and achieving a more democratic future for the people of the
DRC.

7.1. THE ROLE OF INTERNATIONAL ACTORS

The Democratic Republic of Congo (DRC) has a troubled history marked by dictatorship, civil war, and political instability. The country has struggled to establish a functional democracy, and external actors have played a significant role in shaping the political landscape. This section considers the role of international actors in promoting democracy in the DRC, focusing on the United Nations, the European Union, and the African Union.

The United Nations has been involved in the DRC since the 1960s, and its role has evolved. In the early years of the country's independence, the UN provided peacekeeping forces to help stabilize the new state. The UN has recently promoted democracy, human rights, and good governance. For example, the UN helped to mediate the 2002 peace agreement that ended the Second Congo War, and it has supported the country's electoral processes, including the 2018 presidential election. The UN has also provided technical assistance to the country's judicial and security sectors to strengthen the rule of law.

The European Union (EU) has also promoted democracy in the DRC. The EU has provided funding for electoral processes and technical assistance to the country's electoral commission. The EU has also funded civil society organizations promoting human rights and good governance. In addition, the EU has supported efforts to combat corruption and promote transparency in government.

The African Union (AU) has significantly promoted democracy in the DRC through its diplomatic efforts and peacekeeping missions. The AU has been involved in efforts to mediate political conflicts in the DRC, including the 2016 political crisis that followed the end of President Joseph Kabila's second term. The

AU has also supported the country's electoral processes, including the 2018 presidential election.

Despite the efforts of these international actors, democracy in the DRC remains fragile. The country faces significant challenges, including weak institutions, corruption, and ongoing violence in some parts of the country. International actors can play a role in addressing these challenges, but ultimately, the success of democracy in the DRC will depend on the efforts of the Congolese people themselves. Civil society organizations have an important role to play in promoting accountability and transparency in government, as well as in advocating for the rights of marginalized groups. At the same time, political leaders in the DRC must be committed to democratic principles and willing to work together to build a functional democracy.

The World Bank has provided development assistance to the DRC, supporting economic growth and poverty reduction efforts. The bank has also promoted good governance, infrastructure development, and private-sector investment. The bank has identified the potential of the DRC's natural resources to drive economic growth and has supported the country's efforts to manage these resources more effectively.

However, the impact of the World Bank's efforts in the DRC has been limited due to the country's weak governance structures, lack of accountability, and the persistence of corruption. Critics argue that the bank's approach has been too focused on promoting economic growth without adequately addressing the root causes of poverty and inequality in the country.

In 2019, the World Bank approved a $500 million grant to support the country's education system. The grant is aimed at improving access to quality education, especially for girls and disadvantaged groups. The World Bank has also been involved in initiatives to promote economic development and reduce poverty in the DRC.

Despite the efforts of these international organizations, some critics argue that they have not done enough to support the DRC. For example, some have criticized the UN peacekeeping mission for failing to prevent violence in the country. Others have argued that the World Bank and other organizations have focused too much on economic development and not enough on promoting democracy and human rights.

In conclusion, the role of international actors in promoting democracy in the DRC has been significant, but there is still much work to be done. The UN, the EU, and the AU have all played important roles in supporting the country's electoral processes and in promoting human rights and good governance. However, the success of democracy in the DRC will ultimately depend on the efforts of the Congolese people and the willingness of political leaders to work together to build a functional democracy.

7.2. THE FUTURE OF THE DEMOCRATIC REPUBLIC OF THE CONGO

The future of the Democratic Republic of the Congo (DRC) is uncertain, with a complex mix of political, economic, social, and security challenges that pose significant obstacles to sustainable development and stability. Despite these challenges, there are opportunities for positive change, and the international community has a crucial role in supporting the country's transition to a more peaceful and prosperous future.

One of the main challenges facing the DRC is the need to address the root causes of conflict and instability, particularly in the country's eastern regions. This will require a comprehensive approach that addresses local communities' underlying social and economic grievances and efforts to strengthen governance and improve security. The government has taken some steps in this direction, including the establishment of a new peacekeeping force and efforts to engage with armed groups, but much more needs to be done.

Another key challenge is diversifying the economy and reducing dependence on natural resources, particularly mining. The DRC is one of the world's richest countries regarding natural resources, but this has not translated into broad-based economic growth or development for most of the population. Efforts to promote agricultural development and support the growth of small and medium-sized enterprises could help create new employment opportunities and reduce poverty.

There is also a pressing need to address the country's governance challenges, including corruption and weak institutional capacity. This will require reforms to strengthen the rule of law, promote transparency and accountability, and improve public service delivery. The international community can play a role in supporting these efforts through targeted assistance and technical support.

In terms of the political landscape, the recent election of President Felix Tshisekedi in 2019 has raised hopes for a new era of stability and democratic governance. However, there are also concerns about the continued influence of former president Joseph Kabila and his supporters and the potential for further political instability and violence. The international community can support efforts to promote a peaceful and inclusive political transition while also working to ensure that the voices of civil society and opposition groups are heard.

Looking ahead, the future of the DRC will depend on a range of factors, including the success of ongoing peace and development efforts, the ability of the government to address the root causes of conflict and instability, and the degree of support provided by the international community. While the challenges facing the country are significant, there are also opportunities for positive change, and with sustained effort and cooperation, the DRC can realize its potential as a prosperous and democratic nation.

To address these challenges and realize the country's potential, the DRC will need sustained support and engagement from the international community. This support should be based on a shared commitment to sustainable development, good governance, and respect for human rights. Key areas of focus should include:

- Improving governance and combating corruption: This will require strengthening institutions and promoting transparency and accountability in all sectors of the economy and government. Reforms should focus on improving the management of natural resources, including mining and forestry, and ensuring that revenues from these sectors are used to benefit the country as a whole.

- Promoting economic development and job creation: The DRC needs to diversify its economy beyond mining and agriculture and encourage the development of new industries. This will require improving infrastructure, including roads, ports, and airports, and investing in education and skills development to support entrepreneurship and innovation.

- Strengthening security and promoting peace: The government needs to address the ongoing security threats posed by armed groups in the east and ensure that all parts of the country are able to benefit from development. This will require a comprehensive approach, including military and political strategies, as well as support for the demobilization and reintegration of former combatants.

- Ensuring environmental sustainability: The DRC needs to balance economic development with environmental sustainability by promoting responsible mining practices, protecting forests and biodiversity, and addressing the impacts of climate change.

- Investing in social services: The government needs to ensure that all citizens have access to basic services, including healthcare, education, and clean water. This will require significant investment in infrastructure and human resources.

In conclusion, the DRC faces significant challenges in realizing its potential for development and stability. However, with sustained support and engagement from the international community, the country can address these challenges and build a prosperous and sustainable future. It is in the interest of the DRC and the global community to work towards this goal and ensure that the country's vast resources and potential are harnessed for the benefit of all.

7.3. THE ROLE OF YOUTH AND WOMEN IN SHAPING THE COUNTRY

The Democratic Republic of Congo (DRC) has one of the largest youth populations in Africa, with over half of the population under 18. The role of youth and women in shaping the future of the DRC cannot be overstated, given their significant numbers and potential impact. However, these groups face several challenges that hinder their participation in decision-making processes and limit their potential impact.

One of the primary challenges facing youth in the DRC is limited access to education and employment opportunities. Many young people in the country lack basic education and skills, making it difficult to find employment and contribute meaningfully to society. This situation has been exacerbated by years of conflict and instability, which have disrupted education and other essential services. Additionally, young people in the DRC often face social and cultural barriers that limit their participation in political and economic activities.

Women in the DRC also face significant challenges, particularly regarding gender inequality and violence against women. Despite constitutional provisions guaranteeing gender equality, women in the DRC are underrepresented in decision-making positions, and their rights are often violated. Violence against women, including sexual violence, is prevalent in the country, and perpetrators often go unpunished. The situation is particularly dire in conflict-affected areas, where women and girls are often targeted for sexual violence.

Despite these challenges, both youth and women in the DRC have demonstrated their resilience and determination to make a difference in their communities and country. Youth-led movements, such as Lutte pour le Changement (Lucha) and Filimbi, have advocated for democracy, good governance, and social justice. Women's organizations, such as the Association des Femmes des Médias (AFEM) and Women's Platform for the Central African Forests (RECAO), have been instrumental in promoting women's rights and empowering women in their communities.

Harnessing the potential of youth and women in shaping the future of the DRC

Several measures need to be taken. Firstly, there is a need for increased investment in education and skills training for young people to improve their employability and enable them to contribute meaningfully to society. Secondly, efforts must be made to eliminate gender-based violence and promote gender equality in all spheres of life. This includes increasing the representation of women in decision-making positions, ensuring their access to education and economic opportunities, and promoting their participation in political and civic activities.

Thirdly, there is a need for greater recognition and support for youth and women-led organizations and movements. These groups have demonstrated their ability to mobilize and effect change in their communities but often face limited resources and access to decision-making spaces. Supporting these groups can help ensure that the voices and perspectives of youth and women are heard in shaping the future of the DRC.

In conclusion, the role of youth and women in shaping the future of the DRC cannot be ignored. These groups have significant potential to contribute to the country's development and democratic process. However, several challenges need to be addressed to enable them to realize their full potential. Through investment in education and skills training, promotion of gender equality, and support for youth and women-led organizations, the DRC can harness the potential of these groups and build a brighter future for all its citizens.

7.4. **CASE STUDIES OF SUCCESSFUL DEMOCRATIC TRANSITIONS**

Democratic transitions in Africa have been a topic of discussion for decades. Many African countries have been plagued by authoritarianism, military rule, and a lack of democratic governance. However, some African countries have managed to make successful democratic transitions. This section examines case studies of successful democratic transitions in other African countries and applies the lessons learned to the Democratic Republic of Congo (DRC).

Successful Democratic Transitions in Other African Countries:

South Africa: South Africa's transition from apartheid to democracy in the 1990s is considered one of the most successful democratic transitions in Africa. The transition was led by Nelson Mandela, who advocated for a peaceful transition to democracy. The country's democratic constitution was drafted and adopted in 1996, providing a framework for a multi-party system, free and fair elections, and protection of human rights.

The success of South Africa's democratic transition can be attributed to several factors. First, a broad-based social movement mobilized support for democratic change. Second, the international community, particularly the United States and Europe, provided significant support and pressure for democratic reforms. Third, the new government established a Truth and Reconciliation Commission to address the legacy of apartheid, which helped to promote healing and reconciliation.

Lesson for DRC: The DRC could learn from South Africa's transition by advocating for a peaceful and inclusive transition to democracy. The country needs to establish a democratic constitution that provides a framework for democratic governance, political pluralism, and the protection of human rights.

Ghana: Ghana's transition to democracy in 1992 was another successful democratic transition in Africa. The transition was led by Jerry Rawlings, who became the country's first democratically elected president. The country has since held multiple democratic elections, demonstrating the country's commitment to democratic governance.

The success of Ghana's democratic transition can be attributed to several factors. First, there was a broad consensus among political actors and civil society groups that democracy was necessary for the country's development and stability. Second, the international community, particularly the United States and European Union, provided significant support and pressure for democratic reforms. Third, the military regime had relatively weak control over society and institutions, allowing for a relatively smooth transition.

Lesson for DRC: The DRC could learn from Ghana's transition by strengthening its democratic institutions, promoting political pluralism, and fostering a culture of democratic governance. This would require the country to reform its electoral laws, promote freedom of the press, and ensure the independence of the judiciary.

Tunisia: Tunisia's transition to democracy in 2011 is one of the most recent successful democratic transitions in Africa. A popular uprising against the authoritarian regime of President Zine El Abidine Ben Ali initiated the transition. Establishing a national unity government and adopting a new democratic constitution facilitated the country's transition to democracy.

Lesson for DRC: The DRC could learn from Tunisia's transition by promoting civic participation, strengthening civil society, and ensuring transparency and accountability in government. This would require the country to promote freedom of expression, strengthen anti-corruption measures, and promote civil society organizations' active participation in governance.

Conclusion: Successful democratic transitions in Africa provide valuable lessons for the DRC as it seeks to transition to a democratic government. The country must strengthen its democratic institutions, promote political pluralism, and foster a culture of democratic governance. The lessons learned from successful democratic transitions in other African countries provide a roadmap for the DRC to follow in its quest for democratic governance.

7.5. THE POTENTIAL CONSEQUENCES OF IGNORING THE DEMOCRATIC REPUBLIC OF THE CONGO

The Democratic Republic of the Congo (DRC) is a country of immense importance to Africa and the world. The country is home to a wide range of mineral resources, including cobalt, copper, and diamonds, which are vital to many industries, such as technology, renewable energy, and manufacturing. Additionally, the world's second-largest river by volume, the Congo River, provides hydroelectric power to much of the country and the region. However, the DRC faces numerous challenges threatening its stability and ability to contribute to the world. Ignoring these challenges could severely affect the country and the global community.

One of the most significant potential consequences of ignoring the DRC is the exacerbation of conflicts within the country. The DRC has been in conflict for decades, with various armed groups fighting for territory, resources, and power. This conflict has led to numerous human rights cases of abuse, including the use of child soldiers, rape, and other forms of violence against civilians. Ignoring the situation in the DRC could lead to a further escalation of the conflict, which would not only have devastating consequences for the Congolese people but could also destabilize the entire region.

Another potential consequence of ignoring the DRC is its impact on the global economy. As previously discussed, the DRC is home to a wide range of mineral resources vital to many industries. Any disruption to the production and export of these resources could have severe consequences for global supply chains, resulting in increased costs and potential shortages. Moreover, ignoring the DRC's economic and social issues could increase poverty, inequality, and corruption, leading to further instability and potentially affecting regional trade and investment.

The DRC's environmental issues also have the potential to impact the world. Deforestation, mining, and climate change all contribute to environmental degradation within the country, which has consequences for biodiversity and climate. The Congo Basin is home to the second-largest tropical forest in the world, which plays a vital role in mitigating the effects of climate change by absorbing carbon dioxide from the atmosphere. Ignoring the DRC's environmental issues could lead to further deforestation and damage to this vital ecosystem, exacerbating climate change and having global consequences.

Finally, ignoring the DRC could have severe humanitarian consequences. The country has one of the highest rates of poverty in the world, with millions of people living in extreme poverty. Moreover, the country is prone to natural disasters, including floods and disease outbreaks, which could have devastating consequences for the population. Ignoring the situation in the DRC could result in increased suffering and hardship for the Congolese people.

In conclusion, ignoring the challenges facing the Democratic Republic of the Congo could have severe consequences for both the country and the global community. The potential exacerbation of conflict, economic instability, environmental degradation, and humanitarian crises could all have significant global consequences. Therefore, the international community must pay attention to the situation in the DRC and take action to address the challenges facing the country.

7.6. WORKING TOWARDS SUSTAINABLE DEVELOPMENT IN THE DRC

The Democratic Republic of the Congo (DRC) is a country with immense potential for growth and development. However, given its history of conflict, economic instability, and environmental degradation, it will require significant support from the global community to achieve its full potential. Addressing these issues will also require a concerted effort from the global community, including international organizations, governments, businesses, and civil society.

Economic Solutions — One key solution to the DRC's economic challenges is promoting sustainable investment in the country. This can include investments in key sectors such as mining, agriculture, and energy. Sustainable investments will help create jobs and boost economic growth while ensuring that natural resources are managed sustainably.

Additionally, efforts should be made to promote regional integration in the DRC, including improving transport infrastructure and increasing cross-border trade. This will help create a more integrated and competitive regional market, benefiting both the DRC and its neighbours.

Social Solutions: Efforts should be made to promote inclusive economic growth and to improve access to basic services such as healthcare and education. This can be achieved through targeted social programs, including cash transfers, school feeding programs, and community health initiatives.

Additionally, efforts should be made to promote gender equality and empower women and girls in the DRC. This can include initiatives to increase women's participation in political and economic decision-making processes and programs to improve access to education and healthcare for women and girls.

Environmental Solutions: Efforts should be made to promote sustainable land use practices and to protect forests and other natural resources. This can be achieved through initiatives such as REDD+ (Reducing Emissions from Deforestation and Forest Degradation), which provides financial incentives for countries to reduce their greenhouse gas emissions by conserving and restoring forests.

Additionally, efforts should be made to promote sustainable energy solutions in the DRC, including investments in renewable energy sources such as solar and wind power. This will help reduce greenhouse gas emissions and improve access to electricity for the population.

Governance Solutions: Efforts should be made to strengthen democratic institutions and promote good governance. This can include initiatives to improve the transparency and accountability of government institutions, as well as programs to promote human rights and the rule of law.

Additionally, efforts should be made to combat corruption and promote transparency in managing natural resources. This can include initiatives to improve the mining sector's transparency and accountability and reduce illegal mining activities.

International Support: it is also important that the global community provides the necessary support and resources to the country. This can include financial assistance, technical expertise, and capacity-building programs.

International organizations such as the United Nations and the World Bank can play a key role in supporting the DRC, as can other countries and regional organizations. Additionally, private sector engagement can also play a role, with businesses supporting sustainable development initiatives in the country.

To address the complex issues facing the DRC, a multi-faceted approach is required, involving both national and international efforts. The following are some strategies that could be implemented to promote sustainable development in the country:

Strengthening governance and the rule of law: The DRC's government needs to prioritize efforts to improve governance and the rule of law to reduce corruption and improve transparency. This would create a more enabling environment for foreign investment and improve the country's economic situation.

Encouraging responsible foreign investment: Foreign investment can be critical in supporting the DRC's economic development, but it should be done responsibly. Investors must respect human rights and environmental protections while ensuring local communities benefit from projects.

Promoting sustainable agriculture: Agriculture is a major source of employment and income for many Congolese, and sustainable agricultural practices can help protect the environment and increase productivity. This includes promoting crop diversification, improving soil fertility, and using agroforestry practices.

Investing in renewable energy: Investing in renewable energy could help reduce the DRC's dependence on fossil fuels while improving access to energy for the country's population. The country has significant potential for hydropower and solar energy, which could be harnessed for sustainable development.

Supporting conservation and biodiversity: The DRC's forests are a vital resource for the country and the world, providing important ecosystem services and hosting a high level of biodiversity. Efforts to protect and conserve these forests should be a priority, including implementing policies to reduce deforestation, promoting sustainable land use, and supporting eco-tourism growth.

Promoting regional cooperation: Many of the issues facing the DRC, such as conflict and the exploitation of natural resources, are cross-border issues. Regional cooperation could help address these issues and promote sustainable development, including promoting regional trade and investment and addressing common.

8. Conclusion

In conclusion, the Democratic Republic of the Congo is a complex and multifaceted country with a rich history, diverse culture, and vast potential. However, it also faces significant political instability, social inequality, economic underdevelopment, environmental degradation, and resource exploitation.

As we have explored in this book, neglecting the DRC's problems can have far-reaching consequences for the country and the global community. The impact of the DRC's mineral resources, environmental issues, and social and political instability can be felt worldwide, affecting industries ranging from technology to renewable energy.

The international community must actively support the DRC's sustainable development, including investing in economic diversification and creating job opportunities, promoting good governance and human rights, and mitigating the environmental impact of mining and deforestation.

The future of the DRC is bright, but it will require concerted effort and collaboration between the government, the private sector, civil society, and the international community to achieve its full potential. By working together, we can ensure that the DRC becomes a thriving and prosperous country, contributing positively to the world and its people.

The Democratic Republic of the Congo has a rich history and vast potential. Yet, it faces numerous challenges regarding political instability, social inequality, economic development, environmental degradation, etc. The global community needs to recognize the importance of the DRC, not only for its abundant natural resources but also for its role in African and global affairs.

Efforts must be made to address the DRC's issues, including corruption, conflict, and environmental degradation. Sustainable development must be a priority, and this can be achieved through effective governance, investment in education and healthcare, diversification of the economy, and support for environmental conservation efforts.

Ultimately, the future of the DRC depends on the actions taken today. With the right policies, investments, and partnerships, the DRC can overcome its challenges and realize its potential as a leading African nation.

9. Glossary

1. **Coltan** — A metallic ore that is a tantalum source used in electronic devices such as smartphones and laptops. The Congo has significant reserves of coltan, which has been a major driver of conflict and exploitation in the country.

2. **Congo Crisis** — A period of political upheaval and conflict in the Democratic Republic of Congo from 1960 to 1965, characterized by multiple secessions, foreign intervention, and violence.

3. **Ebola Virus Disease** — A severe and often fatal disease caused by the Ebola virus, which is endemic to parts of Africa, including the Democratic Republic of Congo. The country has experienced multiple outbreaks of Ebola, with the largest outbreak occurring from 2018 to 2020.

4. **Joseph Kabila** — The son of Laurent-Désiré Kabila, who succeeded his father as president of the Congo in 2001 and served until 2019.

5. **Joseph Kasavubu** — The first President of the Democratic Republic of Congo, who served from 1960 to 1965. He played a key role in the country's struggle for independence from Belgium, but was ousted in a coup in 1965.

6. **Katanga** — A province in southeastern Congo with rich mineral resources declared secession in 1960 and was the site of intense fighting during the Congo Crisis.

7. **Kinshasa** — The capital city of the Democratic Republic of Congo, located on the Congo River in the southwestern part of the country.

8. **Laurent-Désiré Kabila** — A Congolese revolutionary and politician who overthrew Mobutu Sese Seko in 1997 and served as president of the Congo until his assassination in 2001.

9. **Lumumba, Patrice** — The first democratically elected Prime Minister of the Congo, who served briefly in 1960 before being overthrown in a coup and later assassinated.

10. **M23 Rebellion** — An armed rebellion in the eastern part of the Democratic Republic of Congo, which began in 2012 and was led by the M23 rebel group, consisting mostly of soldiers who had previously been integrated into the Congolese army.

11. **Mobutu Sese Seko** — The long-ruling president of the Congo (then Zaire) from 1965 to 1997, known for his authoritarian regime, extensive corruption, and lavish lifestyle.

12. **Rwandan Genocide** — A mass killing of an estimated 800,000 Tutsis and moderate Hutus in Rwanda in 1994, which had significant spillover effects in neighbouring countries, including the Congo.

13. **Second Congo War** — A conflict that lasted from 1998 to 2003, involving multiple armed groups and neighbouring countries and resulting in an estimated 5 million deaths, making it one of the deadliest wars since World War II.

14. **UN peacekeeping mission** — A military intervention by the United Nations to help maintain peace and security in the Congo, which has had a significant presence in the country since the end of the Congo Crisis in the 1960s.

15. **Transitional Government** — A government formed after a period of conflict or political transition, intended to provide stability and facilitate the transition to a more permanent form of government. The Democratic Republic of Congo has had several transitional governments in its history.

10. References

De Villers, C. (2006). The heart of the Congo: Political risk in a fragile state. Journal of International Affairs, 60(1), 179-197.

Edgerton, R. (2002). The troubled heart of Africa: A history of the Congo. St. Martin's Press.

Englebert, P. (2009). Africa: Unity, sovereignty, and sorrow. Lynne Rienner Publishers.

Gondola, C. D. (2009). The history of Congo. Greenwood Press.

Hochschild, A. (1999). King Leopold's ghost: A story of greed, terror, and heroism in colonial Africa. Houghton Mifflin Harcourt.

Kabemba, C., & Kambala, K. (2010). Congo in limbo: The transition and the failure of democracy. International Journal of Conflict and Violence, 4(1), 84-98.

Nzongola-Ntalaja, G. (2014). The Congo from Leopold to Kabila: A people's history. Zed Books.

Prunier, G. (2009). Africa's world war: Congo, the Rwandan genocide, and the making of a continental catastrophe. Oxford University Press.

Stearns, J. (2011). Dancing in the glory of monsters: The collapse of the Congo and the great war of Africa. PublicAffairs.

Turner, T. (2013). The Congo Wars: Conflict, myth and reality. Zed Books.

Van Reybrouck, D. (2015). Congo: The epic history of a people. Harper Collins.

Vlassenroot, K., & Raeymaekers, T. (2004). Conflict and social transformation in Eastern DR Congo. World Development, 32(11), 1877-1893.

Wemakoy Okia, O. (2016). The Democratic Republic of the Congo: From Leopold to Kabila. Palgrave Macmillan.

Wembi, M. (2009). The Congo's road to democracy: A critical appraisal. The Journal of Modern African Studies, 47(3), 397-416.

Young, C. (2018). The politics of transition in the Democratic Republic of Congo. African Affairs, 117(469), 174-196.

Printed in Great Britain
by Amazon

25958236R00076